LL 60

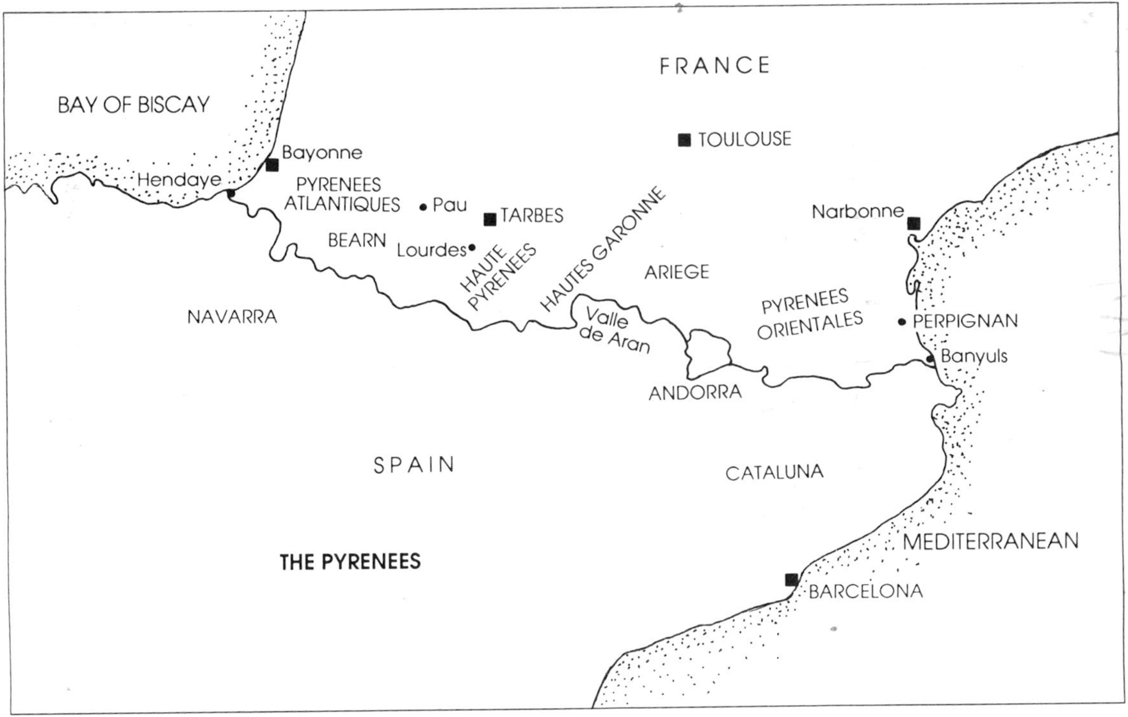

THE PYRENEES

THE PYRENEAN TRAIL GR10

COAST TO COAST ACROSS THE FRENCH PYRENEES

by

ALAN CASTLE

CICERONE PRESS, MILNTHORPE, CUMBRIA

ISBN 1 85284 245 8
Revised Edition 1997

"Adventures such as this make men boys again; the enthusiasm of youth returns. What a grand thing enthusiasm is! How glorious to be alive when your blood is afire!"

A. Wainwright
A Pennine Journey

FOR MY PARENTS

* * *

ACKNOWLEDGEMENTS

The author would like to thank his wife for all her encouragement during the planning and writing of this guidebook, and for the correction of the final manuscript. Andrée Cain gave much needed assistance with the French language. Special thanks must go to Alan, Greta and Kevin Hall for updated details of parts of the route and for a fine selection of photographs of the western half of the GR 10. Thanks are also due to the many hikers of various nationalities who shared various sections of the path with the author whilst he surveyed the trail over two long summers. Finally the author is indebted to the numerous holidaymakers, locals and gîte and refuge guardians who offered advice, assistance and encouragement.

The author is also most grateful to the several users of the first edition of this guidebook who provided updated information on the state of the Trail and facilities en route, in particular to Bruce Logan, Nigel Milius and Peter Mungall.

CONTENTS

SECTION 1: PAYS BASQUE

SECTION 2: BEARN

SECTION 3: HAUTES PYRENEES

SECTION 4: HAUTE GARONNE

Vignemale North Face and Glacier des Oulettes
Section 3 Variant - Day 1

ADVICE TO READERS

Readers are advised that whilst every effort is taken by the author to ensure the accuracy of this guidebook, changes can occur which may affect the contents. A book of this nature with detailed descriptions and detailed maps is more prone to change than a more general guide. New fences and stiles appear, waymarking alters, there may be new buildings or eradication of old buildings. It is advisable to check locally on transport, accommodation, shops etc, but even rights-of-way can be altered, paths can be eradicated by landslip, forest clearances or changes of ownership. The publisher would welcome notes of any such changes for future editions.

By the same author:

Tour of the Queyras (French and Italian Alps)
Walking in the Ardennes
The Robert Louis Stevenson Trail (Cévennes, France)
Walks in Volcano Country (Auvergne and Velay, France)
The Corsican High Level Route
Walking the French Gorges (Provence and the Ardèche)
The Brittany Coastal Path

INTRODUCTION

THE PYRENEES

Stretching from the Atlantic Ocean in the west to the Mediterranean in the East, a distance of some 250 miles (402.5km), the mountains of the Pyrenees form a natural barrier between Spain and the Iberian Peninsula in the south and France in the north. The range contains several peaks above 3000m (9,852ft) in altitude, the highest of which is the Pico d'Aneto (3,404m; 11,179ft) on the Spanish side of the border. The Pyrenees do not form a continuous line of mountains, but rather two principal chains of approximately equal length. The western chain rises from the Bay of Biscay and runs slightly south of east for about 125 miles (201km). The eastern chain overlaps the western chain by about 7 miles (11km) and also runs south-eastwards to end at Cape Cerbère on the Mediterranean coast.The two chains overlap east of Bigorre at the Val d'Aran where the River Garonne flows over from Spain into France. For the most part the watershed is traced by the political frontier, along which many of the highest and most spectacular peaks are to be found. However there are substantial massifs on either side of the border, particularly on the Spanish side. The major summits from west to east are Pic d'Anie, Pic du Midi d'Ossau, Balaïtous, Vignemale, Monte Perdido, Pico de Posets, Pico de la Maladetta, Pico d'Aneto, Encantados, Pic d'Estats, Pic Carlitte and Pic du Canigou.

The geology of the Pyrenees is very complex, but the principal rocks are limestone and granite. In geological terms these mountains are modern, being formed by the same earth movements that produced the Alps some 50-100 million years ago in the Tertiary period. The present-day features have been largely brought about by glacial action and this is particularly the case on the northen side of the mountains where there are many glaciated valleys, pyramidal peaks and sharp arêtes. There was once a great ice sheet covering much of the area with a front of nearly 200 miles (322km) pushing northwards over a great distance. However, the southerly latitude and the influence of Mediterranean air-streams have slowly caused a recession of the ice and today only a few small glaciers are left. The largest remaining glacier is the Ossoue Glacier on Vignemale.

Several dramatic cirques are a feature of the Pyrenean landscape, where valley heads end abruptly in precipitous walls forming a horse-shoe shaped corrie. The best known of these is at Gavarnie.

There are well over two thousand glacial lakes in the Pyrenees and these add greatly to the beauty of the landscape. However there are no large natural lakes in these mountains, the longest being under 2 miles in length (Lac de Lanoux, near the Carlitte massif). Several larger man-made lakes have been constructed to provide hydro-electric power.

There are noticeable differences between the north and south sides of the mountains, and also between the western and eastern regions of the chain. The northern or French side has relatively high precipitation resulting in fertile valleys with steep north-facing slopes. The southern side tends to be much drier and the hills run out gently to the Spanish plain. The western end of the chain is affected by Atlantic air-streams and precipitation is fairly high. Oak and pine forests are commonplace in the west, whereas in the east the vegetation is influenced by the dry Mediterranean climate and orchards and vineyards are the norm. The central high Pyrenees provide an Alpine climate and associated flora.

GR 10

The GR 10 is one of a number of official long distance paths (Grandes Randonnées) in France. The GR system is very extensive and some 25,000+ miles (40,250+km) of footpath have been designated and waymarked. Each GR route has been allocated a number. The GR 10 runs from Hendaye on the west coast through the mountains of the Pays Basque, Béarn and Hautes Pyrénées to Luchon. From here it continues generally in an easterly direction to pass the sparsely populated Ariège, then across the Pyrénées Orientales to end on the Mediterranean coast at Banyuls-sur-Mer. The total distance is some 538 miles (866km). Throughout its length the GR 10 remains in France, although at times it actually follows the Franco-Spanish border. A variety of landscapes is traversed from woodland to Mediterranean scrub, from high pasture to rocky ridges. Even though the GR 10 excludes the major summits of the Pyrenees, walking this trail involves a considerable amount of ascent and descent (some 156,000ft; 47,500m) and navigational skills are required to cross often wild and remote areas. The GR 10, which celebrated its 21st anniversary in 1996 (i.e. 21

years since the complete trail was opened), is a coast-to-coast mountain walk par excellence.

There is another route which traverses the Pyrenees from west to east, the High Level Route or Haute Randonnée Pyrénéene (HRP). This generally keeps to the highest ground possible and frequently crosses over to the Spanish Pyrenees. Unlike the GR 10 the HRP is not waymarked (except on a few sections) and a high level of navigational ability and good general mountaineering skills are required. There is a guidebook written in English to this route (see Bibliography).

CLIMATE

The Pyrenees lie in the south-west of France at around latitude 43°N, so it is not surprising that summers tend to be rather warm. Humidity can sometimes be high and violent thunderstorms are not uncommon. As in all mountains, temperatures decrease with altitude. Temperature, wind speed and cloud base can change rapidly so local weather conditions within the mountains often show great variation. Within the space of a few days the author has experienced temperatures in the upper 30's (centigrade), torrential rain, high winds and a 3-inch snow-fall!

The western Pyrenees show features of an Atlantic weather system, with cloudier skies and higher precipitation than in the eastern mountains which are influenced by warm, dry Mediterranean air. In the central Pyrenees there is a zone of transition between the western and eastern climates, and here altitude and aspect have a great effect on weather conditions.

The area of permanent snow is small in the Pyrenees because of the southerly latitude, limited altitude and exposure to mild air-streams from the Mediterranean. During the warm summers snow vanishes from all but the highest summits and north-facing cirques. In winter snowfall can be considerable; the observatory on the Pic du Midi de Bigorre records a depth of 20 feet of snow during most years. All the passes are usually blocked and many of the high villages isolated. The mountains of the central Pyrenees are snow-covered above 4,000ft (1,218m) for an average of a 100 days per year, although this period of snow cover is much less in the eastern Pyrenees. The snow line retreats rapidly in early summer and avalanches and swollen torrents are widespread.

WHEN TO GO

The extreme ends of the Pyrenean chain, from Hendaye to Saint-Jean-Pied-de-Port in the west and from Arles-sur-Tech to Banyuls-sur-Mer in the east, could probably be walked at any time of the year. This is particularly true of the eastern section where any snow is unlikely to linger. In the central Pyrenees snow is likely to persist on the high cols until well into June. Hence the most favourable time of year to walk the GR 10 would be from about mid-June until the end of September, before the first winter snows appear. The arrival of summer and the melting of the snows can come rather late in some years, so parties venturing out in mid-June and even early July could still find parts of the route blocked by snow.

Most French people take their holidays between Bastille Day (July 14th) and the Feast of the Assumption (August 15th). During this period the refuges and gîtes d'étape may possibly be somewhat crowded, particularly in the more popular areas. However, unlike the Alps, overcrowding is unlikely to be a serious problem in the Pyrenees.

Virtually everyone returns to work by September in France, so certain summer-only facilities, along with some refuges, may close by then. The more sparsely populated and less well-known areas (such as parts of the Ariège) are likely to be very deserted by September, thus adding to the objective danger for anyone travelling alone or in a small group.

TRAVELLING TO THE PYRENEES

Excluding the use of private transport (which is impractical when walking a linear route) there are four main ways of travelling to the Pyrenees.

(1) AIR

There are four destinations worthy of consideration.

Biarritz (for the western end of the Pyrenees; Pays Basque.)

Air France operate direct flights from London, Heathrow to Biarritz, but only during the months of July, August and September. British Airways only offer an indirect flight from the UK via Paris, Charles de Gaulle airport. The passenger then has to transfer to Paris, Orly airport for an Air Inter flight to Biarritz. Apex fares are available.

Lourdes (for the central Pyrenees; Pic du Midi d'Ossau; Gavarnie.)

Once again the British Airways route is via Paris, with a connecting Air Inter flight from Paris, Orly to Lourdes. Lourdes is a popular place of pilgrimage and several charter companies offer flights from a number of British airports. Your local travel agent should be able to provide further information.

Toulouse (for the Ariège and central Pyrenees.)

Air France from Heathrow offers direct flights to Toulouse five times per week (Apex fare available). British Airways flights are via Paris. There are also four flights daily by Air Inter to Paris.

(All of the above services are liable to cancellation or alteration at any time.)

(2) TRAIN

The train is probably the most useful and versatile form of transport for those planning a walking holiday in the French Pyrenees. French trains are generally fast, punctual, clean, comfortable and not overly expensive. A journey to the Pyrenees from London can be completed by train in under 24 hours. Unlike air travel where one is normally required to return to the same airport for the journey home, when travelling by train one can simply go to the nearest railway station at the end of the walk and return from there.

There are frequent services to Hendaye (via Bordeaux and Bayonne) at the western end of the GR 10, and to Banyuls-sur-Mer (via Perpignan) at the eastern end. There is also a very convenient service to Luchon (Bagnères-de-Luchon), the half-way stage of the GR 10. Other major rail lines serving the Pyrenees are to Pau, Lourdes, Tarbes and Toulouse. A few of these destinations can be reached direct from the Channel ports, but in most cases it will be necessary to change trains in Paris. Trains from the Channel ports arrive in Paris at the Gare du Nord or Gare Saint Lazare and it will be necessary to travel across Paris from there to Gare d'Austerlitz (or Gare de Lyon). The Métro (Paris Underground) is the most convenient way to do this. Most destinations in the Pyrenees and their environs are reached from Gare d'Austerlitz, but services to Perpignan and the Mediterranean coast also operate from the Gare de Lyon. It is now possible to take the Eurostar service from Waterloo International through the Channel Tunnel direct to Gare du Nord (Paris), where, as before, you must transfer to Gare Austerlitz. This can now be done using the RER service which is faster than the ordinary metro.

Travel Centres in major British Rail stations in most large cities in the UK can supply timetable and price information, book tickets and make seat and couchette reservations. A seat/couchette reservation is advisable if travelling during the peak holiday season (particularly at weekends). Note, however, that SNCF reservations will only be accepted within two months of your travel date. The French Railway Office in London (see Useful Addresses) can also be of assistance and on request will supply details of various concessionary fares and holiday passes.

One cautionary note. Access to railway station platforms is free in France, but tickets must be validated by date stamping before boarding the train. This simple task is performed using the orange coloured machines which are located on the concourse of nearly all French railway stations. Failure to do this can result in a fine.

(3) COACH

There is not an extensive network of long distance coaches in France comparable to that in the UK. However there are two long distance coach routes that are of use to the GR 10 walker.

(i) **London (Victoria coach station) to Saint-Jean-de-Luz**

From here it is a short train journey to Hendaye at the start of the GR 10. There are up to seven coaches per week in both directions during the main summer season. Coaches run from the beginning of April to the end of September. Journey time is about 21 hours.

(ii) **London (Victoria) to Perpignan**

From Perpignan it is a short train journey to Banyuls-sur-Mer at the eastern end of the GR 10. A daily service in both directions operates from the beginning of April to the end of September. Journey time is about 22 hours.

These two services probably offer the cheapest means of travelling to and from the Pyrenees, but are usually less comfortable than the train. They are direct (although several stops are made en route) and luggage deposited in the coach at the start of the journey need not be retrieved until the destination has been reached, with the exception of carrying it through British Customs on returning to the UK.

There is also a frequent and inexpensive coach service from London to Paris which operates several times a day. This could be used to reach the Pyrenees in combination with a French train.

Details of all of these services (operated by Eurolines) and tickets can be obtained from National Express offices and agents.

(4) FERRY
Another possibility is to travel by ferry from Plymouth to Santander in Spain. This might be convenient for walkers living in the south-west of England, or for those wishing to see the Spanish side of the Pyrenees before commencing the GR 10. The service is run by Brittany Ferries and operates twice weekly in both directions (sailing time about 24 hours). It would then be necessary to take a train from Santander to Hendaye to commence the GR 10.

LOCAL TRANSPORT
In general the public transport network in the Pyrenees is rather sparse. Several of the towns and villages that once boasted a railway station are now dependent on a local bus service or have no public transport facilities at all. In some areas there is a bus service (often a SNCF bus, ie operated by the National Railway Company) which links the more inaccessable villages with the nearest railway station.

The main possibilities for local public transport are given below, but remember that these services are liable to change and cancellation at any time. On many of these routes part of the journey is by rail and the remainder by connecting bus.

(1) Bayonne —> Guéthary —> Saint-Jean-de-Luz —> Hendaye-Plage —> Henday-Ville —> Irun.
(2) Bayonne —> Ossés —> Saint-Etienne-de-Baïgorry or Saint-Jean-Pied-de-Port.
(3) Pau —> Oloron-Sainte-Marie —> Bedous —> Lescun —> Etsaut —> Urdos —> Canfranc.
(4) Pau —> Busy —> Laruns.
(5) Lourdes —> Pierrefitte-Nestalas —> Luz-Saint-Sauveur —> Barèges or Pierrefitte-Nestalas —> Cauterets —> Gavarnie.
(6) Tarbes —> Bagnères-de-Bigorre —> La Mongie.
(7) Tarbes —> Lannemezan —> Saint-Lary —> Bourisp —> Arreau.
(8) Toulouse or Tarbes —> Bagnères-de-Luchon.
(9) Toulouse —> Boussens —> Saint-Girons.
(10) Toulouse —> Pamiers —> Foix —> Ax-les-Thermes —> Mérens-les-Vals —> L'Hospitalet —> La Tour-de-Carol—> Andorra.

(11) Perpignan —> Le Soler —> Vinca —> Prades —> Villefranche-de-Confluent —> Thuès-les-Bains —> Planès —> Mont Louis —> La Tour-de-Carol.
This is the picturesque Train Touristique called the Petit Train Jaune (little yellow train).

(12) Perpignan —> Argelès-sur-Mer —> Pont Vendres —> Banyuls-sur-Mer —> Cerbère —> Port-Bou.

Details of these services can be obtained from the UK office of SNCF (see Useful Addresses).

If no bus or train is available it is likely that there will be a taxi service in the locality. Tourist offices or even the local bar/café should be able to provide details of taxi services. The only other alternative is to hitch a lift from a passing motorist. It is relatively easy to obtain lifts in the Pyrenees as the local people are generally helpful, being aware themselves of the problems caused by the lack of public transport. Much of the traffic is local and therefore one shouldn't expect to travel large distances by this means, but rather to be taken to a place where public transport is available.

Finally it is useful to understand the road classification in France. French A-roads are autoroutes (motorways). N or RN (route nationale) roads are equivalent to British A-roads. D or département roads are equivalent to British B or C-roads.

EQUIPMENT

A lightweight sleeping bag is essential for the backpacker and highly recommended for those walkers making use of gîte d'étape and refuge accommodation. Not all gîtes d'étape and few of the refuges supply blankets, and the cabanes have only a wooden sleeping area. Most walkers find a heavy 3/4 season sac to be unnecessary for much of the time in these southerly latitudes, although it can be sometimes fairly cold at altitude at night, even during the height of summer.

For much of the time shorts and a tee-shirt will be the most comfortable attire, but warm clothing should be carried to allow for the possible deterioration in the weather and for evening use. A waterproof and windproof jacket is essential and many people would also wish to carry waterproof trousers. A pair of thin gloves weigh very little and could save discomfort if the weather turns cold at altitude. Rather than carry the heavy weight of traditional breeches it may be preferred to pack a pair of lightweight walking trousers which can be worn on the occasional cool day, or to protect sensitive skin against sunburn. Such trousers can also be worn whilst relaxing in the evenings.

The glare and heat from the sun can be intense, particularly during July and August and at altitude. The use of a sunhat, high factor suncream and lip-salve will all help to avoid over exposure to the sun. Sunglasses may also be useful. To ensure that fluid is readily available during the day, at least one 1-litre bottle should be carried per person. Mineral water is often sold in screw-cap plastic bottles in France and these can provide useful additional water carriers.

Well worn-in boots are essential for this walk. Some type of lightweight shoe is also desirable for rest days and for relaxing in the evenings. A pair of good quality trainers is recommended as these can be used as an alternative form of footwear on easy sections of the route. Note that in general boots are not permitted inside refuges and gîtes d'étape.

A small first-aid kit is important as there will only be the occasional opportunity to buy simple medicines whilst en route. Include plasters, antiseptic cream, safety pins, a small bandage, aspirin/paracetamol and anti-diarrhoea tablets. Insect repellent may also be found useful. The first-aid box is a good place to store a whistle; it can then easily be located in an emergency.

There are several miscellaneous items that may be of use. A small torch is invaluable in navigating a route across a sea of slumbering bodies in a crowded refuge. A small French/English dictionary or phrasebook may help with communication. A small Swiss army knife or similar implement will provide a sharp blade for cutting (eg bread, salami), a pair of scissors, a can opener and a cork-screw.

The rucksack is probably the most important item to be carried. It is vital to inspect the sack thoroughly for wear before leaving for France. Try to ensure that the carrying mechanism is not likely to break whilst on holiday. Apart from injury this is the worst fate that can befall the walker, particularly in an area such as the Pyrenees, where the possibility of repair or replacement is remote. A dustbin-liner for the rucksack and a supply of plastic bags should keep equipment dry in heavy rain. Equipment is best packed in different coloured stuff sacks to enable easy identification and access to various items. The author generally uses one stuff sack for spare clothes, one for kitchen equipment and one for maps, guidebooks, writing paper etc. Perishable food is best kept in a disposable plastic bag to prevent the accidental soiling of the inside of the rucksack.

The backpacker will need to carry additional equipment. A small lightweight tent will be the main requirement. A closed-cell type of insulating mat will cut down body heat loss through the ground and will also give added comfort in several of the cabanes where there are no mattresses, only a wooden sleeping area. A stove will be necessary; probably the most convenient to use in France during the summer months is the Camping Gaz variety. Spare gaz canisters are easily obtainable in France at many of the places along the GR 10, although these are several walking days apart in some areas. Methylated spirits (alcool à brûler) and lead-free petrol can also be purchased in France. If travelling by air it is important to remember that none of these fuels can be carried on board an aircraft; they will have to be purchased on arrival in France. A small cooking set will also be required and if carrying a Swiss army knife or similar, then the only item of cutlery really necessary is a spoon. Don't forget a box of matches or a lighter!

A rope will not be required on any part of the GR 10 provided that the walker does not stray from the route. Similarly neither ice-axe nor crampons should be necessary during the summer months, although the possibility of freak weather covering the high passes with snow and ice can never be ruled out. Moreover, in some years snow and ice can be very late in clearing from several of the high passes. Outside the main summer months an ice-axe and crampons would be essential items of equipment. Many continental mountain walkers use telescopic walking poles. British walkers may also find these useful, particularly on long, steep sections.

OVERNIGHT ACCOMMODATION

The equipment required for the walk depends largely on whether you intend to backpack (carrying tent, stove and cooking utensils) or make use of gîte d'étape, refuge, cabane or hotel accommodation every night. Obviously the chief advantage of the latter is that far less weight need be carried and indeed it is perfectly possible to walk much of the GR 10 in this way. This guide has been designed so that some form of permanent shelter is available at the end of each daily stage. Many of the gîtes d'étape and refuges provide cooked meals and most of them have equipped kitchens where food may be prepared.

Remember, however, that in certain areas (eg from Gestiès to Mérens-les-Vals in the Ariège) there are very long stretches without habitation or guarded refuges. Here the unguarded cabanes provide the only form of shelter. Note that occasionally cabanes are destroyed (eg by fire, avalanche or vandalism), locked or converted to animal use, in which case the walker without a tent could face a serious problem. If the itinerary described in this guidebook is followed, then ten nights in all would be spent in unguarded cabanes. These are all in the eastern half of the Pyrenees (Section 5, the Ariège, and Section 6, the Pyrénées Orientales). All other nights would be spent in either gîtes d'étape, guarded refuges or in hotels.

The main danger of relying on accommodation is that if one's destination is not reached by nightfall, then a night out in the open may be necessary and this could have serious consequences in bad weather without proper equipment. For this reason it is recommended that anyone not carrying full backpacking equipment should include some form of survival bag in his or her rucksack.

The backpacker, although carrying an extra burden, has greater freedom each day and is not restricted to reaching a gîte d'étape or hut each night. It will, however, be necessary to locate a water supply and find a suitable place to camp, a task not always easy in these often steep-sided mountains.

Backpacking can of course provide a cheaper holiday than gîte or refuge 'hopping', but only if all the necessary equipment is already owned.

GITES D'ETAPE

These are the simple hostels found all over France along the GR trails which provide basic and cheap accommodation for the walker. In the Pyrenees they have been established by an organisation called Randonnées Pyrénéennes whose logo is an upright walking bear carrying a walking stick. This sign is often used in villages or towns to indicate the route to the gîte d'étape. Their location is marked on IGN maps. Gîtes d'étape (not to be confused with gîtes rural which are rented holiday homes) provide convenient overnight accommodation along much of the GR 10. There are many gîtes d'étape along the route, although the aim of establishing them at distances no more than a day's walk apart along the trail has not yet been realised. However the many gaps in the gîte d'étape system can usually be filled with mountain refuges or cabanes.

Gîtes d'étape come in all shapes and sizes from converted barns or stables to large houses or parts of hotels. Few are purpose built. The wardens are often farming folk who use the gîte d'étape as an extra source of income. The typical gîte d'étape will accommodate between ten and thirty people in a unisex dormitory, usually on large mattresses. Its kitchen will be equipped with stoves and cooking utensils and there will also be a dining area. There are usually hot showers as well as washbasins and toilets. The warden often does not reside in the gîte d'étape but may live in an adjacent farm or house. Meals are often provided by the guardian and these generally represent good value for money.

It is not necessary to be a member of any organisation to stay at a gîte d'étape. They are inexpensive and a standard fixed rate is operated by the gîtes d'étape affiliated to the Randonnées Pyrénéennes. They are primarily intended for walkers travelling along the GR trails and under normal circumstances one is not encouraged to stay any longer than a few days at any one gîte. They make ideal bases in which to sit out a spell of bad weather. Sometimes a small fee is payable for use of the gîte during the daytime.

Gîtes d'étape tend to be cheaper than mountain refuges, and as many of them are situated in villages or small towns there will often be shops and other facilities available. They can on occasions become very crowded and, although the warden will seek to accommodate everyone, late arrivals may have to go elsewhere. Overcrowding of gîtes d'étape is, however, less of a problem in the Pyrenees than it is in the Alps. It is possible to book ahead by telephone, although this is often impracticable and rarely necessary. Arriving early at a gîte d'étape is the best way of reserving a bed for the night.

The Randonnées Pyrénéennes is an organisation devoted to improving the facilities in the Pyrenees for the walker, and new gîtes d'étape are being opened all the time. Occasionally a gîte d'étape will close down. Many of them are only open during the main season from mid-June to mid-September. It is a good idea to keep abreast of the current situation. Information about neighbouring gîtes d'étape will often be posted up in the gîtes; otherwise ask the guardian if there are any new gîtes d'étape along the next section of the trail. The wardens are usually eager to help and are a good source of local information. Before leaving England it might be advisable to write to the

Randonnées Pyrénéennes who will supply the latest information on all gîtes d'étape, refuges and cabanes in the French Pyrenees. Enclose an International Reply Coupon (see Useful Addresses). Expect to pay about 55-60FF for an overnight at a gîte d'étape and around 80FF for a night at a refuge.

MOUNTAIN REFUGES

Whereas gîtes d'étape tend to be situated in villages or small towns, accommodation in the mountains themselves comes in the form of mountain huts or refuges. These are virtually the same as those found in the Alps, and indeed many of them are owned and run by the French Alpine Club (CAF). Their location is marked on IGN maps. They are usually substantial buildings of stone and/or wood with unisex dormitories, a kitchen/dining room/sitting room and toilets. Many of them have their own generator. For the simple accommodation provided the charges are quite high, but then one is paying for facilities in a remote mountain location. There are reductions for members of CAF and for members of affiliated Alpine Clubs, but unless many nights are to be spent in refuges the cost of membership will not be recouped. The British Mountaineering Council can supply information concerning membership of various Alpine Clubs (see Useful Addresses).

Most refuges have a resident guardian during the summer months and it is important that on arrival a bed-space is immediately booked with him/her. It is rarely possible to book in advance and places are allocated on a first-come, first-served basis. During the main season the most popular refuges can become very crowded, but it is unusual for a late arrival at a full refuge to be turned away, although it may be necessary to sleep on the floor.

Meals are provided at some of the refuges, although they are often poor value for money compared with the cost of meals in the valleys. It will be necessary to carry a stove and cooking utensils if self-catering as such equipment is seldom provided in refuges. Hot water is not usually available and any shower available is likely to be connected to a cold water source! Not all refuges are in the high mountains and a few are to be found with public road access (eg the CAF refuge at the Barrage des Bouillouses in the Pyrénées Orientales). In these the amenities tend to be less spartan. Whatever the situation, a night spent in a mountain refuge can be a novel experience!

The majority of mountain refuges are only fully open with a resident warden during the main summer months, although several have a second high season during the winter by providing accommodation for skiers or winter mountaineers. When the main refuge is closed (commonly from mid-September onwards) there will usually be a small annex or 'winter room' left permanently open to provide shelter and overnight accommodation. The facilities available here are fairly primitive and similar to those of the cabane (see below).

CABANES

Cabanes or abris (shelters) are small buildings, usually a single room of stone construction. Neither electricity nor piped water is supplied. They are found in the most isolated parts of the mountains and are most numerous on the eastern half of the GR 10. In one four-day section in the Ariège they provide the only form of permanent shelter. There is no guardian and the sleeping area is often no more than a raised wooden platform. They often have a fireplace which can make for a cosy evening, provided that there is sufficient dry wood in the vicinity. There is sometimes a crude table and a few chairs or benches. Despite the spartan nature of the accommodation, staying in cabanes in the Pyrenees can be a pleasurable experience particularly if shared with a small group of friendly people.

There are a few private cabanes which are kept locked, but most are left open and can be used by anyone. Occasionally a shepherd may be living there during the summer and then it would only be possible to stay the night if invited. It would be well to remember that changes do occur in these mountains and a cabane that has been left open for many years may suddenly be locked or reserved for the use of shepherds only.

Cabanes are marked on IGN maps sometimes as 'Cab' and occasionally as 'Cne', or alternatively they appear as 'Abri'. Many cabanes are now marked on the maps using a special symbol (note the Key to Symbols on your map). Lastly, and rather confusingly, some cabanes are referred to as refuges.

HOTELS, DORTOIRS, AUBERGES

All of the towns on the GR 10 and some of the villages have hotel accommodation. Hotels in France are star graded on a system very similar to the one in use in Britain. The basic hotel is the one-star establishment and this is usually reasonably priced, clean and comfortable. A list of hotels can usually be obtained from the local Syndicat d'Initiative (Tourist Information Office).

Sometimes hotels or restaurants have associated outbuildings or attics. These 'dortoirs' will provide cheaper but more basic accommodation for the night. Some villages whilst not boasting a hotel may have an auberge, a simpler sort of establishment often with rooms above a café / restaurant.

OFFICIAL CAMPSITES

There are several official campsites on the route of the GR 10. It will be necessary to provide passport details and complete a registration form.

Although camping is extremely popular in France, tents tend to be of the large frame variety and the French have not taken enthusiastically to backpacking. Therefore a small backpacking tent will often be squeezed in between large family tents. Many campsites in France are extremely well equipped, with bars, restaurants, sports facilities, hot showers etc. However large family groups often make a lot of late night noise.

WILD CAMPING

The Pyrenees offer one of the finest wilderness camping areas in Europe and wild camping (camping sauvage) is to be recommended. It will be necessary to find a pitch well away from habitation and roads. The art of wild camping is to ensure that no trace of an overnight stop is left; all litter must be removed, great care should be taken with matches and stoves and water sources must not be polluted.

Wild camping is not permitted within the boundaries of the National Park.

WESTERN PYRENEES NATIONAL PARK

There is one National Park situated within the French Pyrenees. This is the Parc National des Pyrénées Occidentales which consists of a large, albeit irregularly shaped area that extends eastwards from the region south of Lescun to the Néouvielle massif south of the Col du Tourmalet. Within its boundaries are some of the most impressive mountains in the Pyrenees, including the Pic du Midi d'Ossau, Balaïtous, Vignemale and the Cirques of Gavarnie and Troumouse.

The Park, created in 1967, is an area safeguarded against commercial exploitation and forms a sanctuary for the natural flora and fauna of these mountains. It contains no permanent human habitation. The GR 10 passes through the Park in the region of the Pic du Midi d'Ossau, and again on the recommended alternative route from Cauterets to Luz-Saint-Sauveur via Gavarnie.

WAYMARKING AND NAVIGATION

The GR 10, like all the GR trails in France, is waymarked in its entirety with a system of red and white painted stripes. These occur, usually in a horizontal position with white above red, on rocks, boulders, trees, posts, fences, telegraph poles etc. In some areas of the Pyrenees through which the GR 10 passes, there are other painted markings in a variety of colours and forms. Some of these are waymarks for local nature trails, forest walks and the like; some mark the route to a mountain summit while others refer to hunting areas or horse riding trails. The most confusing are red or orange-red marks which occur without a white stripe. Always remember that it is only red and white stripes occurring together that mark the GR trail.

Various arrangements of red and white lines are used to signify different instructions. When two sets of red/white marks appear together it signifies that a change in direction is imminent. This instruction is also sometimes indicated by the use of 'bent' red and white markings curving in the new direction to be taken. The painted cross, usually of one red and one white line is an important one to remember: it signals that the route is not in that direction and you must go back to pick up the correct trail. Very occasionally a red and white mark bisected by another white line may be observed. This does not necessarily mean that a mistake has been made, but rather that this route is a variant of the main GR trail.

Many of the cols and other high places are marked with a signpost providing the name of the area and its altitude. In addition several small, metal GR 10 signposts will be seen indicating the direction and time to the next village or town. Most of these have been erected by the local Maison du Tourisme.

Other notices may sometimes be seen. 'Propriété Privée' or 'Défense d'Entrer' means that the area is private and entry forbidden. The signs 'Reserve du Chasse' and 'Chasse Privée' do not refer to walkers, but indicate that hunting rights are reserved for the owner of the land.

The overall standard of waymarking on the GR 10 in the French Pyrenees is not particularly high when compared with many trails in the French Alps. In certain areas the waymarks are fresh, well placed and easily interpreted, but in others they may be very faded, non-existent or placed very far apart. Hence vigilance is required at all times. One should always remember that the marking of GR trails is done by volunteers, and the French have many thousands of miles of GR path to maintain. Some work on trail marking takes place every summer; so an area difficult to negotiate because of poor markings in one year could present no problems the following summer.

In the more popular areas of the French Pyrenees, such as in the vicinity of the Pic du Midi d'Ossau in the west and around Pic du Canigou in the east, the paths are well used and easy to follow. In the main season there are usually plenty of other walkers and day trippers to be found here. However in certain other regions, and in particular in the Ariège, there are few places of habitation and the paths are little used. In these areas navigation is sometimes quite tricky and the route is often unclear on the ground. Hence the ability to use a map and compass correctly is essential when walking much of the GR 10. Although the true route of the GR 10 involves very little scrambling, if the walker goes astray in these large mountains far more dangerous ground may be encountered. If in doubt always go back to the last red and white waymark and start again.

MAPS

The IGN (Institut Géographique National), the French equivalent of our own Ordnance Survey, publish a series of special maps at 1:50,000 covering the whole of the French Pyrenees. Ten of these maps (Carte de Randonnées, édition Randonnées Pyrénéennes) are required to cover the whole route from the Atlantic Ocean to the Mediterranean Sea. The GR 10, the High Level Route and other GR walking tours in the Pyrenees are marked on these maps. Refuges, campsites, gîtes d'étape and cabanes are all clearly marked. The maps required are as follows (west to east):

Map no 1- Pays Basque Ouest
2 - Pays Basque Est
3 - Béarn
4 - Bigorre
5 - Luchon
6 - Couserans-Val d'Aran
7- Haute-Ariège-Andorre
8 - Cerdagne-Capcir
10 - Canigou
11 - Albères-Roussillon.

Note that Map no 9 (Montségur) in the series is not required for the GR 10.

It is essential to purchase only the most up-to-date maps as older editions can show parts of the route which have been abandoned by the FFRP in favour of a new section, eg south of St. Jean Pied de Port and east of the Refuge du Ruhle.

These maps can be purchased from Stanfords in London, or from other specialist map dealers in Britain (see Useful Addresses).

If planning to complete the whole route of the GR 10 in one holiday, it might be sensible to post home each map as it is used in order to reduce the weight carried. It would even be possible to post some of the maps not required in the first stages of the GR 10 from home to post-offices en route, then collect them by calling at the relevant post-office whilst on the walk.

The IGN also produce maps at 1:100,000 (Serie Verte) and four of these maps are required to cover the whole of the Pyrenean chain (nos 69-72). Although the route of the GR 10 is marked on these maps, they are really only useful for initial route planning as they have insufficient detail for use in the field.

MOUNTAIN SAFETY

The well equipped and well prepared walker who is sufficiently skilled in the use of map and compass should encounter no particular problems whilst walking the GR 10. However the Pyrenees are high and remote mountains, so some experience of walking in mountain country should be obtained before venturing into them. A knowledge of basic mountain safety precautions and emergency procedures should also be gained before setting out on the route.

In common with other mountain areas, sudden changes in the weather can and do occur. Always keep an eye open for weather changes and never hesitate to turn back or head for the nearest shelter if conditions deteriorate. Plan ahead, look for possible escape routes to be used in an emergency, never overestimate your physical ability and always carry plentiful reserves of food. Fatigue, slight injury or losing time because of navigational errors could all result in a failure to reach the day's intended destination. For this reason some form of survival bag should be taken if a tent is not carried.

Never be afraid to ask the wardens of the huts or gîtes d'étape for a weather forecast or other advice. They are usually more than willing to oblige. Other walkers, particularly those who are walking the route in the opposite direction to yourself, are another good source of information about the state of the path ahead.

The walker should know the International Distress Signal, viz six audible (eg whistle) or visual (eg torch) signals for one minute followed by a minute's silence. The alarm is then repeated. The answer from a party coming to the rescue is three such signals followed by a minute's pause. Help can also be summoned by using arm signals: raising both arms high in the air means 'I require assistance'; one arm raised and the other lowered means 'I do not need assistance'. In the Pyrenees, as in other European mountains, it is only advisable to summon the rescue services if it is absolutely essential. It is an extremely costly business (see Insurance).

FOOD

Except in a few cases, where advice is given in the relevant section, the walker on the GR 10 is usually within a day's walk of at least one grocer's shop. In rural areas shops tend to offer a limited choice of provisions. In the larger villages and towns bread is sold in a boulangerie (or dépôt du pain); cakes, pastries and biscuits in a pâtisserie; cold meats, sausages and pâté in a charcuterie and groceries in an épicerie or alimentation. These shops tend to open earlier than their equivalents in Britain (usually around 7.30-8.00am) and stay open later (often up to 8.00pm). The big snag is that they close for much longer than a lunch 'hour'. A walker arriving in a village any time between noon and 3.30pm is likely to find the shops closed. Provisions can sometimes be purchased from the guardian of a gîte d'étape which is particularly useful when there is no shop in the immediate locality.

Dehydrated meals are difficult to obtain in the Pyrenees and therefore should be purchased in Britain if required. However French packet soups are very good, and a wide variety is on sale everywhere. When supplemented with pasta and perhaps saucisson sec or cheese, soup can provide a fairly substantial meal. Fruit, vegetables, cheese, cold meats and sausages are excellent and widely available. Milk is usually of the UHT variety and sold in litre disposable containers. The commonest form of bread is the baguette which, although tasty, will become very stale within a few hours. Longer lasting wholemeal bread is becoming more readily available in France and is generally more suitable on a walking holiday.

It is sometimes possible to avoid the heat of the day by taking a long relaxing lunch in a restaurant or café. (Note that a snack at lunchtime will probably cost almost as much as a full meal.) Evening meals in French restaurants are generally of a high quality and reasonably priced, but often not available until 7.00-7.30pm. Breakfasts consist only of coffee (or drinking chocolate) with bread and jam. Many restaurants double as bars/cafés and will often serve drinks to customers not requiring a meal.

WATER

In general water sources are plentiful along the GR 10. However there are certain sections where water will not be found for several hours and so a full water bottle should be carried whenever possible. Areas where water is particularly scarce are mentioned in the text. The heat in these southern latitudes in the summer can be intense and heat exhaustion and dehydration may rapidly develop when carrying heavy loads on steep mountainsides. Always ensure that an adequate quantity of liquid is consumed.

Many of the water sources are safe to drink, but of course one can never be sure, particularly if there are cattle, sheep or goats in the vicinity. If in doubt add a water purifying tablet to any unboiled water, allowing at least 10 minutes for the chemicals to react before drinking the water. Water labelled 'L'Eau Non Potable' is not suitable for drinking.

FIRE

The combination of southerly latitude, hot often dry summers and lush vegetation results in the constant threat of forest and other fires. These are more likely to occur on the hotter and drier Mediterranean side of the Pyrenees. Common sense will help avoid a catastrophe. Extreme caution should be exercised when using matches, lighters and in particular gas or liquid fuel stoves.

WILDLIFE

The Pyrenean chamois or isard is common in these mountains, but like their Alpine equivalents they are shy creatures and seldom seen at close range. Although marmots are not native to the Pyrenees, many will be seen and heard. Mountain goats are also fairly common. Reports in recent years have suggested that the European brown bear still survives in the Pyrenees, but one will be very fortunate indeed (or very unlucky!) to sight a specimen. Another very rare but interesting creature is the desman, a rat-like mammal living in streams and marshy areas whose only other European habitat is the Caucasus. Mice are not uncommon in some of the mountain cabanes and refuges! Therefore protect your foodstuffs.

There are plentiful frogs and toads to be found and many lizards will be seen flitting across the hot rocks during the heat of the day. A colourful salamander may occasionally be observed. Vipers and certain other snakes are common in many areas (see below).

Several species of birds of prey live in the Pyrenees. Eagles and vultures are of particular interest and may be observed riding the thermals high up above the mountains. Vultures are most likely to be encountered in the Basque region of the Pyrenees.

The combination of three factors, a southerly latitude, an Alpine-type environment and relatively little interference from man (to date) has resulted in a great wealth and variety of plants and flowers in the Pyrenees. Both Alpine and Mediterranean species are found, while nearly two hundred species are endemic to the Pyrenees. Alpine flowers abound and in particular the gentians, crocuses, orchids and the Pyrenean asphodel are a delight to observe in their mountain habitat. Wild fruits are common and in the right season raspberries and strawberries will provide a free supplement to a walker's diet.

VIPERS

Unfortunately vipers or adders are fairly common in the Pyrenees and a bite, although unlikely to be fatal, could have serious consequences in the remote areas of the mountains where help is not quickly available. Fortunately they are quite secretive animals, likely to detect a walker's presence by vibrations along the ground and take avoiding action. Nevertheless keep a good lookout for vipers in order to avoid accidentally treading on one. The chances are that the GR 10 will be completed without catching sight of even one of these reptiles.

If bitten it is necessary to rest, avoid a panic reaction, get medical help as soon as possible and in the meantime try to suck out the venom. It is possible to buy an aspiratory device for this purpose in pharmacies in France. This aspirator consists of a syringe with various sized and shaped attachments which enables venom to be sucked from a wound. It is also possible to purchase a viper venom antidote (antiserum) without prescription in French pharmacies. The application of this requires a self-injection in muscle tissue near the site of injury, but it should only be used in absolute emergencies where medical help cannot be obtained (see also Insurance).

INSURANCE

It is advisable to take out travel and medical insurance for the duration of the holiday as rescue and hospitalisation charges are very expensive in France. Several companies issue cover for hill walking, rambling, scrambling and camping (ie activities excluding the use of specialist equipment such as ropes and ice-axes). Take the original copy of the insurance with you to the Pyrenees, but leave a photocopy with a relative or friend at home.

There are certain reciprocal rights available for British subjects in France under National Health Service arrangements within the EEC. Information concerning eligibility for medical cover under this scheme and the necessary E 111 form can be obtained from local DHSS offices.

HEALTH AND FITNESS

It is important to stay as healthy as possible whilst walking a long distance route such as the GR 10. Even a minor cold can develop into something much more serious if the walker does not rest but continues to heave a heavy rucksack over high mountain passes. Particular care should be taken over personal hygiene; clean all food properly before eating and be wary of drinking contaminated water. Diarrhoea and sickness should be treated immediately with the appropriate tablets, obtainable from any good pharmacist (it is best to buy a few at home and include them in a first-aid kit). Failure to correct these stomach upsets can lead to weakness, dehydration and further complications. If symptoms persist then a doctor should be consulted.

Regular walking in the British hills should help prepare the walker for the GR 10; otherwise some programme of exercise in the months preceding the trip would be sensible. Before travelling to France it would be advisable to undertake a few short backpacking trips in order to become more accustomed to carrying a load. The main difference between walking in Britain and in the Pyrenees is the length of some of the ascents and descents. As one friend new to such walking once told the author "I was unused to starting a climb after breakfast and still be clambering up the same hill at teatime!" On the GR 10 this is a slight exaggeration, but after a few days I think that you will know exactly what he meant!

LANGUAGE

The French, like the British, are not particularly keen on learning foreign languages. Many of the younger people can speak some English, but in general do not expect the level of fluency found in Holland or Germany. In the small communities through which the GR 10 passes, little English will be spoken. It is a good idea to brush up on 'rusty' French before the holiday; even the most elementary grasp of the language will pay dividends by enriching the experience of walking in France. However no true adventurer will be discouraged by an inability to speak the local language, even if it will necessitate the occasional use of sign language!

French is of course the official language, but in the Pays Basque the Basque tongue will also be heard. This is a strange ancient language which is unrelated to any of the Indo-European family of languages. Its grammar is incredibly complex (for instance each noun can appear in thirty-six different variations!) but fortunately nearly all of the Basques north of the border speak French as well as their own language.

MONEY

The only currency required for walking the GR 10 is the French Franc, but remember that for any detours into the Spanish Pyrenees a supply of Spanish Pesetas will be required. It is advisable to carry a fairly large supply of moderately low denomination notes (50,100 and 200FF notes are particularly useful). In several areas through which the GR 10 passes there are no banks or money exchanges for many days (or even longer!), so ensure that sufficient cash is carried. The author has found that Eurocheques are particularly useful, the only problem sometimes being that a minimum quantity will have to be exchanged (1,400FF in 1996). Alternatively traveller's cheques may be carried. French Franc traveller's cheques are the most useful as these can sometimes be used in restaurants, hotels etc as immediate payment. Access and Visa cards are accepted widely in France and are a useful form of payment for restaurant meals and rail tickets.

It must be stressed that money exchange facilities along the GR 10 are not numerous. Normal banking hours are from around 9.00am until midday, and from 2.00-3.00pm until 4.00-5.00pm. Many banks are closed all day Saturday. In the small towns and large villages along the GR 10 where there are banks, they are sometimes only open on one or a few days per week, and occasionally just for a couple of hours! Note that some of the larger post-offices (PTT) will cash Eurocheques.

TO TELEPHONE BRITAIN

It is easy to phone direct to Britain from any public call box in France. The procedure is as follows. Lift the receiver and insert the appropriate coins, after which a dialling tone will be heard. Dial 19 (the code for an international line) and pause until a second dialling tone is heard. Then dial 44 (the code for the UK). Pause again before dialling the STD code of the number required, but minus the initial zero. Lastly dial the number of the line required. For example, to phone a number in Liverpool (STD Code 0151) dial: 19,pause,44,pause, 151 123 4567. In a few small villages (eg Couflens in the Ariège) there are no call boxes, but it is possible to use the telephone in the PTT (French post-office). Ask at the counter and use the public phone indicated. Make the call and then pay at the counter (the call will have been metered). Alternatively it may be possible to use the phone in a hotel, café or restaurant, but it is likely that a call will be more expensive if made in this way.

Many public telephone boxes in the large towns and cities in France will not accept coins and require the use of a phonecard instead. Phonecards can be purchased at most post-offices, but this is usually inconvenient for the visitor. There are now very few coin-operated public telephones in Paris, but in case of difficulty there is one in the station precincts of Gare Saint Lazare (normally with a long queue!).

PUBLIC HOLIDAYS

There are more public holidays in France than in Britain. Fortunately between June and October there are only two to consider, Bastile Day on July 14th and the Fête of the Assumption on August 15th. On both of these days the public transport system is considerably affected and many shops are closed, although most cafés and restaurants stay open. It is well to bear these days in mind and to plan accordingly, particularly if it is necessary to travel by public transport on either of these days.

For most of the year French time is one hour ahead of the time in

In the Gorges de Kakouéta

The path to Pas d'Azuns

Above Bious-Artigues

Britain, ie French summer time is one hour ahead of BST. For a few weeks in late September and early October Britain and France are on the same time (liable to change).

PHOTOGRAPHY

Most walkers will wish to have a photographic record of their journey through the French Pyrenees. The best type of camera to take is probably the 35mm SLR. The use of a wide angle lens (eg 28 or 35mm) is particularly recommended for the type of landscape photography possible in these mountains. A telephoto lens will be useful for capturing details of more distant features. All of this camera equipment is unfortunately very heavy, but a compromise would be to use a medium zoom lens (eg 28-80mm) on a SLR body. This would obviate the need to change lenses continually, but nevertheless zoom lenses are themselves heavier than prime lenses. Weight can be radically reduced by using a good quality 35mm compact camera equipped with a reasonably wide-angled lens, or alternatively a zoom lens. The quality can be almost as good as an SLR camera, but the compact camera is light and small, easily fitting into a pocket.

It is best to purchase all the film required at home before leaving for the Pyrenees. For colour transparencies either 64 or 25 ASA film is suitable, and for colour prints 100 ASA will yield good results. The use of a UV filter is recommended to cancel the blue bias that UV light has on colour film (light at altitude has a strong UV content). Protect both used and unused film from heat by placing it well inside the rucksack. Finally, it is better to take all exposed film home rather than posting it back to Britain to be processed. It could be lost in the post or damaged by X-ray equipment in the sorting offices.

WALKING THE GR 10: VARIOUS SUGGESTIONS FOR WALKING HOLIDAYS OF VARYING LENGTH

To complete the GR 10 in the stages outlined in this guide will take 47-50 days. Most people do not have this sort of time available and consequently will want to walk only part of the route, or alternatively walk the whole of the GR 10 over a number of annual holidays. The major considerations are the time available, the type of landscape preferred and the public transport possibilities. The following itineraries outline a range of different holidays on the GR 10.

Four-Week Holidays

The GR 10 can conveniently be walked over two annual holidays each of about a month's duration.

Holiday 1: Western Pyrenees

Hendaye to Bagnères-de-Luchon. 22-25 days' walking. Luchon has a regular main-line train service to Paris.

Holiday 2: Eastern Pyrenees

Bagnères-de-Luchon to Banyuls-sur-Mer. 25 days' walking.

Two-Week Holidays

To walk the whole length of the GR 10 over a number of annual holidays the following stages are suggested.

Holiday 1

Hendaye to Lescun or Etsaut. 10 or 11 days' walking. From Lescun a SNCF bus can (usually) be taken to Bedous for the train to Pau. Similarly there is a bus service operating from Etsaut to Bedous.

Holiday 2

Lescun or Etsaut to Luz-Saint-Sauveur where there is a bus service to Lourdes (rail to Paris or airplane to Britain). 8 or 9 days' walking if the Tour du Pic du Midi d'Ossau and the Gavarnie variation is included. This would allow time for a thorough exploration of the Pic du Midi d'Ossau area, the Vignemale massif, Cirque de Gavarnie, Cirque de Troumouse etc, as well as providing time for excursions to Pau, Lourdes or Oloron-Sainte-Marie.

Holiday 3

Luz-Saint-Sauveur to Fos (7 days' walking) or Couflens or Saint Lizier d'Ustou (13 days) or Aulus-les-Bains (14 days). Public transport opportunities are not numerous in the Ariège. A taxi would have to be used or other arrangements made to leave the GR 10 to reach Boussens (SNCF train), Saint-Girons (SNCF bus and train) or Foix (SNCF train) for transport to Toulouse (main-line train service to Paris). An occasional bus service may operate from Aulus-les-Bains during the main season.

Holiday 4

Fos/Couflens/Saint Lizier d'Ustou/Aulus-les-Bains to Mérens-les-Vals. 7/8/14 days' walking. Main-line train from Mérens- les-Vals to Ax-les-Thermes and Paris.

Holiday 5
Mérens-les-Vals to Banyuls-sur-Mer. 10 days' walking. This would allow time on a 2 week trip to visit Perpignan and / or Barcelona and relax on the Côte Vermeille.

For those walkers wanting a taste of the Pyrenees but holding no aspirations to complete the whole route, there are numerous possibilities for walking sections of the GR 10, making use of local public transport and then perhaps walking part of a Tour or Variant to reach a convenient valley base. The information in this guidebook should enable the planning of several such trips. The area chosen will depend on the type of landscape preferred and the possibilities for various excursions.

The character of each area can be assessed from the introductory passages that precede each section in this book. However, in summary, go to the Pays Basque to experience a unique culture without the rigours of high mountain walking; go to Béarn and the Haute Pyrénées for the highest and most spectacular of the Pyrenean summits and cirques; go to the Ariège for solitude and unspoilt mountain country and go to the Pyrénées Orientales for the splendours of the Carlitte and Canigou massifs and the warmth of a Mediterranean sun.

Finally, for a short (4-day) circular tour amongst some of the finest mountain scenery in the French Pyrenees I would strongly recommend the circuit of Cauterets—Refuge Bayssellance—Gavarnie—Luz-Saint-Sauveur (Section 3, Variation Days 1-3) followed by Luz-Saint-Sauveur to Cauterets via the Col de Riou (reverse of Day 3, Section 3).

NOTES ON USING THE GUIDEBOOK

Abbreviations

In the table which precedes each Day of the walk, the following abbreviations have been used.

For accommodation:

H	= hotel	CP	= campsite
G	= gîte d'étape	Y	= youth hostel
R	= refuge	A	= auberge
C	= cabane	-	= no facilities

\+ after a symbol indicates more than one such facility

For shops, bars, cafes, restaurants:

+ = facility available
++ = choice of facilities
- = facility not available

Note: when an entry is made both for a hotel under the accommodation column and for a restaurant, the latter may be part of the hotel. Restaurants often double as a bar / café. Many refuges and some gîtes d'étape also serve refreshments and even meals to non-residents.

A symbol in brackets implies that the facility is in the locality but not actually on the route of the GR 10 (where a facility appears in a town or village it may well be some distance from the direct line of passage through that habitation, but in this case it is not placed within brackets. Brief directions to reach such establishments are usually given).

Where a shop is indicated this implies an épicerie (grocer's shop) or supermarket, ie. a place where food may be purchased.

Accommodation

Reference to a refuge (R) generally indicates an establishment with a resident guardian during the main summer season. Meals may or may not be provided. A kitchen with cooking utensils is not normally available.

Reference to a cabane (C) indicates a relatively small building that is unguarded, but left open permanently for shelter or overnight stay. Cooking utensils will not be available.

A gîte d'étape (G) reference means that there is a resident guardian (or one living nearby) and that a kitchen with utensils will usually be available. Meals may or may not be available. A list of gîtes d'étape and refuges on or near the GR 10 and its satellite tours and variants is given towards the end of the book. Telephone numbers are included so that space may be booked a few nights in advance, although this is often not necessary except perhaps in the very popular areas during the main season (note that few guardians speak English!).

Many gîtes d'étape, refuges and even hotels are only open during the main summer season (July and August) and those arriving somewhat early or late may be disappointed.

Distance and Altitudes

Distance and altitudes are given in miles and feet (because most

English-speaking people are more familiar with this system) and also in kilometres and metres (because this is how they appear on the maps).

Note that when altitudes are given in the text these refer to the altitude above sea level of the place in question, not to the amount of climbing required to reach that point. The total amount of ascent and descent for each stage is given at the beginning of each Day.

It is not particularly easy to calculate distances covered on the GR 10 because of the numerous twists and turns on the route and the nature of the terrain traversed. For instance, climbing a hill by thirty tight zig-zags will obviously cover more ground than can be accurately measured on a 1:50,000 map. Generous allowances have been made for the distances stated, so it may be possibly slightly less from A to B than stated but is unlikely to be longer. It is hoped that these distances are close to the actual distance covered on the ground, rather than mere map mileages. However, newcomers to Pyrenean walking will soon realise that altitude gained and lost is a more realistic indicator of the severity of a particular section than the distance to be covered.

Timings

Times as well as distances between the various stages are given. The numbers in the sectional and accumulative timings column in the tables refer to hours and minutes. These times are those that it is considered the average rambler would maintain, but no allowance is made for stopping. The time taken will obviously vary from party to party and depend on the prevalent conditions, but it is often useful to have an indication of the time generally required to walk a section. This is particularly true in the often rugged terrain of the Pyrenean mountains. It is a system widely used in Europe.

Changes

Changes are occurring in the Pyrenees from year to year owing to a variety of factors such as continuing depopulation, increasing numbers of tourists, walkers and climbers visiting the area, and dissatisfaction over a particular section of the GR 10. The main changes affecting the GR 10 wayfarer are as follows:

(1) The opening of new gîtes d'étape, refuges, hotels, restaurants and bars, and the closing of others.

(2) The closing of village shops (the opening of new shops is less likely).

(3) The locking or destruction of cabanes intended as shelters for travellers. The construction of new cabanes.
(4) The reduction or loss of public transport facilities.
(5) Alterations to the route of the GR 10 or the waymarking of new variants.

The author would like to be informed of such changes for inclusion in future editions of this guidebook. Please write with full details via the publisher - Cicerone Press, 2 Police Square, Milnthorpe, Cumbria.

Note that as the Trail of the GR 10 is re-routed from time to time, for various reasons, walkers are always advised to follow the current waymarkings if the route described here is different from that "on the ground" and always to use the most up-to-date IGN maps.

SUMMARY TABLE OF THE GR 10

STAGE	DISTANCE		ASCENT		DESCENT		EST. TIME	
	mls	km	ft	m	ft	m	hr	min
SECTION 1								
1. HENDAYE TO OLHETTE	13.5	21.7	2463	750	2250	685	6	25
2. OLHETTE TO FERME ESTEBEN	20.5	33	3650	1111	1957	596	8	50
3. FERME ESTEBEN TO SAINT ETIENNE-DE-BAIGORRY	17.0	27.4	4537	1381	5909	1799	10	20
4. SAINT ETIENNE-DE-BAIGORRY TO SAINT-JEAN-PIED-DE-PORT	10.5	17.0	2847	867	2864	872	6	15
5. SAINT-JEAN-PIED-DE-PORT TO BEHEROBIE	11.5	18.5	3097	943	2529	770	5	15
6. BEHEROBIE TO COL BAGARGUIAC	14.5	23.7	6046	1841	2772	844	7	30
7. COL BAGARGUIAC TO LOGIBAR								
Route 1	6.5	10.5	397	121	3524	1073	3	55
Route 2	10.0	16.1	1103	336	4230	1288	5	30
8. LOGIBAR TO SAINTE ENGRACE	16.0	25.8	3672	1118	2834	863	7	10
TOTALS FOR SECTION 1	110.0	177.1	26,709	8132	24,639	7502	55	40*

* Totals for Section 1 were taken using Route 1 for Stage 7.

STAGE	DISTANCE		ASCENT		DESCENT		EST. TIME	
	mls	km	ft	m	ft	m	hr	min
SECTION 2								
1. SAINTE ENGRACE TO ARETTE-PIERRE-SAINT-MARTIN	6.5	10.5	3842	1170	525	160	4	35
2. ARETTE-PIERRE-SAINT-MARTIN TO LESCUN	9.0	14.5	1189	362	2962	902	5	00
3. LESCUN TO BORCE	9.0	14.5	2670	813	4148	1263	6	20
4. BORCE TO LAC DE BIOUS-ARTIGUES	13.0	21.0	5215	1588	2696	821	7	30
EXCURSION: Tour du Pic du Mlidil d'Ossau	9.5	15.3	2867	873	2867	873	6	45
5. LAC DE BIOUS-ARTIGUES TO GOURETTE	16.5	26.6	4864	1481	5097	1552	8	55
TOTALS FOR SECTION 2	54.0	87.1	17,780	5414	15,428	4698	32	20*

*Totals for Section 2 omit the Excurtion Tour du Pic du Midi d'Ossau

STAGE	DISTANCE		ASCENT		DESCENT		EST. TIME	
	mls	km	ft	m	ft	m	hr	min
SECTION 3								
1. GOURETTE TO ARRENS	7.5	12.1	1931	588	3468	1056	5	40
2. ARRENS TO CAUTERETS	15.0	24.2	5005	1524	4890	1489	9	50
3. CAUTERETS TO LUZ-SAINT-SAUVEUR	11.5	18.5	3402	1036	4036	1229	6	40
4. LUZ-SAINT-SAUVEUR TO BAREGES	10.2	16.4	2519	767	811	247	5	15
5. BAREGES TO LAC DE L'OULE	12.7	20.4	4391	1337	2483	756	8	15
6. LAC DE L'OULE TO VIELLE-AURE	12.2	19.6	1294	394	4647	1415	6	20
7. VIELLE-AURE TO GERM	8.1	13.0	3793	1155	2023	61	5	05
TOTALS FOR SECTION 3	77.2	124.2	22,335	6801	22,358	6808	47	05

STAGE	DISTANCE		ASCENT		DESCENT		EST. TIME	
SECTION 3 VARIATION								
1. CAUTERETS TO REFUGE BAYSSELLANCE	11.2	18.0	5980	1821	273	83	6	45
2. REFUGE BAYSSELLANCE TO GAVARNIE	11.5	18.5	463	141	4686	1427	6	25
3. GAVARNIE TO LUZ-SAINT-SAUVEUR	13.0	20.9	985	300	3104	945	6	00
TOTALS FOR VARIATION	35.7	57.4	7428	2262	8063	2455	19	10

STAGE	DISTANCE		ASCENT		DESCENT		EST. TIME	
	mls	km	ft	m	ft	m	hr	min
SECTION 4								
1. GERM TO ESPINGO	11.0	17.7	5320	1620	3258	992	7	50
2. ESPINGO TO LUCHON	11.2	18.0	1681	512	6007	1829	6	45
3. LUCHON TO FOS	18.5	29.8	5051	1538	5399	1644	9	35
4. FOS TO ETANG D'ARAING	11.5	18.5	5603	1706	985	300	6	40
TOTALS FOR SECTION 4	52.2	84.0	17,655	5376	15,649	4765	30	50

STAGE	DISTANCE		ASCENT		DESCEN		EST. TIME	
	mls	km	ft	m	ft	m	hr	min
SECTION 5								
1. ETANG D'ARAING TO GRAUILLES	9.0	14.5	3882	1182	6509	1982	8	10
2. GRAUILLES TO CABANE DU TAUS	9.0	14.5	5912	1800	3307	1007	7	55
3. CABANE DU TAUS TO ESBINTS	10.0	16.1	1251	381	4972	1514	6	55
4. ESBINTS TO CABANE D'AULA	10.6	17.1	3314	1009	883	269	5	00
5. CABANE D'AULA TO SAINT LIZIER D'USTO	13.0	20.9	4250	1294	6910	2104	7	55
6. SAINT LIZIER D'USTOU TO AULUS-LES-BAINS	10.3	16.6	3048	928	3015	918	5	25
7. AULUS-LES-BAINS TO MOUNICOU	13.8	22.2	4345	1323	3235	985	8	40
8. MOUNICOU TO GOULIER	14.0	22.5	3905	1189	3829	1166	8	20
9. GOULIER TO SIGUER	7.0	11.3	1442	439	2657	809	4	25

10. SIGUER TO REFUGE DE BALLEDREYT	6.2	10.0	3994	1216	1169	356	5	45
11. REFUGE DE BALLEDREYT TO REFUGE DE CLARANS	4.7	7.6	1225	373	2966	903	3	40
12. REFUGE DE CLARANS TO REFUGE DE PRAT-REDON	11.0	17.7	4296	1308	1869	569	9	05
13. REFUGE DE PRAT-REDON TO MERENS-LES-VALS	9.6	15.5	1793	546	4256	1296	5	30
TOTALS FOR SECTION 5	128.2	206.4	42,657	12,988	45,577	13,878	86	45

STAGE	DISTANCE		ASCENT		DESCENT		EST. TIME	
	mls	km	ft	m	ft	m	hr	min
SECTION 6								
1. MERENS-LES-VALS TO REFUGE DES BESINES 5.5	8.94181		1273	1156	352	4	50	
2. REFUGE DES BESINES TO BARRAGE DES BOUILLOUSES	10.5	16.9	2677	815	2549	776	5	45
3. BARRAGE DES BOUILLOUSES TO REFUGE DE L'ORRY	14.5	23.3	1980	603	2670	813	6	40
4. REFUGE DE L'ORRY TO MANTET	12.0	19.2	3862	1176	4716	1436	7	35
5. MANTET TO MARIAILLES	7.8	12.5	3304	1006	2752	838	5	15
6. MARIAILLES TO CHALET DES CORTALETS (VIA PIC DU CANIGOU)	6.8	11.0	3829	1166	2411	734	5	30
7. CHALET DES CORTALETS TO ARLES-SUR-TECH	15.5	25.0	828	252	6962	2120	6	45
8. ARLES-SUR-TECH TO LAS ILLAS	16.2	26.1	4325	1317	3445	1049	8	30
9. LAS ILLAS TO REFUGE DE LA TAGNAREDE	16.5	26.6	3136	955	1511	460	6	45
10. REFUGE DE LA TAGNAREDE TO BANYULS-SUR-MER	11.0	17.7	1159	353	4591	1398	5	25
TOTALS FOR SECTION 6	116.3	187.2	29,281	8916	32,763	9976	63	00
GRAND TOTALS FOR GR 10 *	537.9	866.0	156,414	47,627	156,414	47,627	321	10

* The grand totals were calculated from the totals for Sections 1-6, omitting the Variation from Cauterets to Luz-Saint-Sauveur via the Hourquette d'Ossoue

INTRODUCTION

Section 1 covers the route of the GR 10 through the Basque region of France from the Atlantic Ocean at Hendaye to the Sainte-Engrâce valley at the eastern extreme. The GR 10 passes through many Basque villages on its journey eastwards, in particular it visits the historic town of Saint-Jean-Pied-de-Port, once an important resting place for pilgrims making the long journey to Santiago de Compostela in north-west Spain. The terrain gradually changes from rolling foothills near the coastal region to the high mountains of the central western Pyrenees. The route is seldom more than a few hours from habitation, and accommodation and re-provisioning should rarely produce problems.

The most interesting feature of this section is the Basque culture evident throughout the walk. One tends to think of the Basques as a fiercely independent group living in north-west Spain, waging guerrilla warfare against the Spanish government in a bid to gain their independence. One often forgets that the territory of the Basques stretches over the border into France. The French Basques are just as independently minded as their Spanish counterparts, but they have not resorted to violent means to express their grievances and so have tended to be somewhat ignored by the outside world. The French Basques (there are about a hundred thousand of them) would consider themselves first and foremost as Basques, and only secondly as citizens of the French Republic. They are nearly all bilingual and fortunately it will not be necessary to grapple with the intricacies of the Basque language. (The written language is interesting to examine, note the abundance of X's and K's.) Many of the place names on the route are Basque in origin, although on the French IGN maps often only the French name is given (for example Sainte-Engrâce is known to the locals by its Basque name, Santazi).

Many other aspects of Basque culture will be evident to the walker. The style of the local architecture is quite different from that of neighbouring Béarn. The farmhouse is the most important building in the Basque community, its size and elegance denoting the status of the occupants. Indeed a Basque takes his surname from the name of his house rather than from his father! One child (usually the eldest) inherits everything.

Nearly every village has in addition to its church a 'fronton' or pelota wall. Pelota is a Basque game played at a furious pace. It has vague similarities with the game of fives but there are no side walls and the ball is caught and thrown with the aid of a basket strapped to one arm. It is played against a wall (the fronton) in a large open-air court, between two teams of three players. It is well worth watching a pelota match - very aggressive but highly entertaining! Exhibition matches are often staged during the annual fête at the fronton in Saint-Jean-Pied-de-Port.

The Basque communities of the Pyrenees have a unique way of life. In some mountain communes a large percentage of the land is held by the village as a whole and members of the individual farmsteads come together during the summer months to tend the flocks of sheep and goats owned by the commune on the high pastures. During this period they live high up in the mountains in the 'olha' or shepherd's summer hut, tending the animals and making cheeses. Some of these olhas (Cayolars in Béarnais) are passed on the GR 10.

The unique way of life of the Basques in their mountain communities, perhaps best illustrated by the commune of Sainte-Engrâce, has remained unchanged for many centuries. Unfortunately the pressures of the 20th century are being felt even here, and now many of the young people spend time away from their mountain homes during the year to earn money to supplement their farm income. The school in Sainte-Engrâce has been facing closure for several years. It will certainly be tragic if this ancient way of life that has survived for so long in the heart of Europe is lost for ever.

Both walkers and conservationists may complain about the large number of dirt tracks in the mountains of the Pays Basque. It is true that in places they have obliterated the trail of the GR 10, but to the Pyrenean shepherds they are of great importance. They have revolutionised the life of these Basque shepherds, allowing rapid movement in the once roadless mountains and greatly facilitating the handling of sheep and the transportation of their large, heavy cheeses made up on the high pastures. So spare a thought for the shepherds who live here when desperately searching for the trail. Nowadays tourists and day trippers will often be seen driving along these 'roads'.

Much of this section does not perhaps have the spectacular scenery

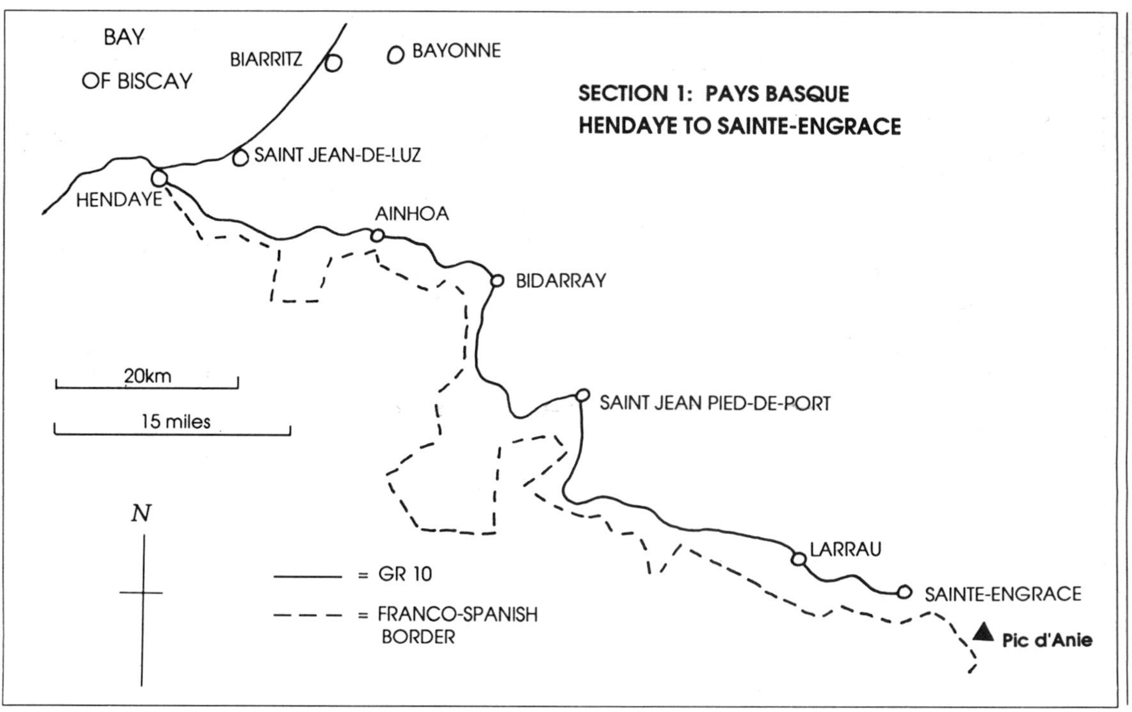
BAY
OF BISCAY
BIARRITZ
BAYONNE
SECTION 1: PAYS BASQUE
HENDAYE TO SAINTE-ENGRACE
SAINT JEAN-DE-LUZ
HENDAYE
AINHOA
BIDARRAY
20km
15 miles
SAINT JEAN PIED-DE-PORT
N
= GR 10
= FRANCO-SPANISH
BORDER
LARRAU
SAINTE-ENGRACE
Pic d'Anie

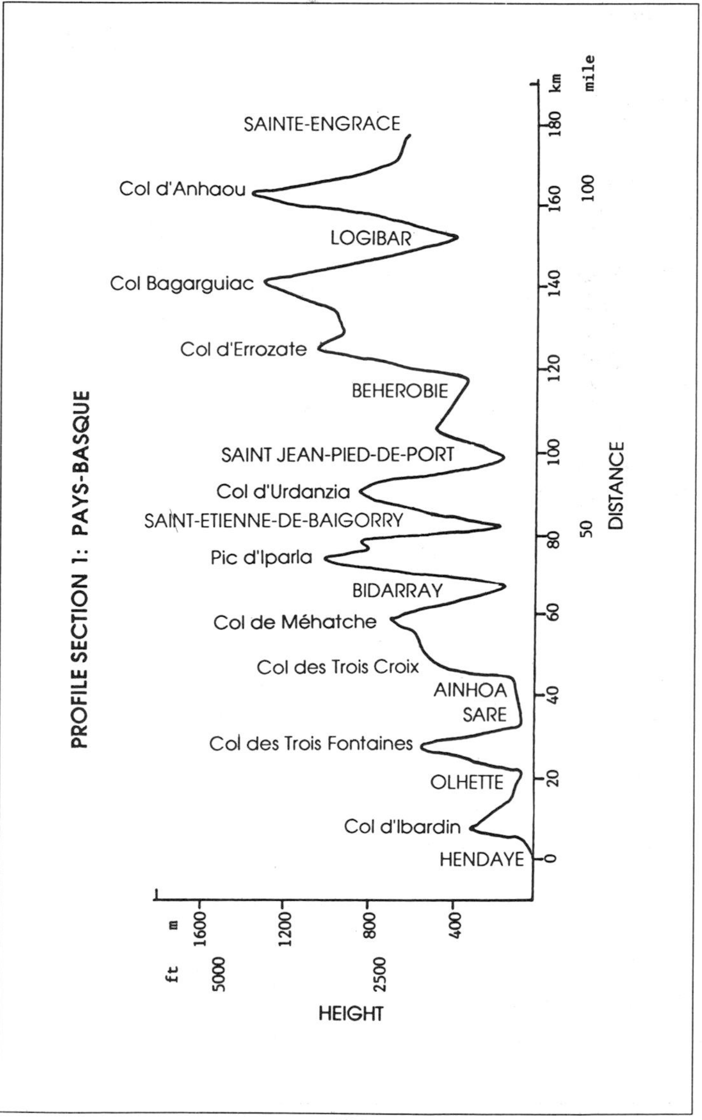
PROFILE SECTION 1: PAYS-BASQUE
SAINTE-ENGRACE
Col d'Anhaou
LOGIBAR
Col Bagarguiac
Col d'Errozate
BEHEROBIE
SAINT JEAN-PIED-DE-PORT
Col d'Urdanzia
SAINT-ETIENNE-DE-BAIGORRY
Pic d'Iparla
BIDARRAY
Col de Méhatche
Col des Trois Croix
AINHOA
SARE
Col des Trois Fontaines
OLHETTE
Col d'Ibardin
HENDAYE
km
0
20
40
60
80
100
120
140
160
180
mile
50
100
DISTANCE
m
1600
1200
800
400
ft
5000
2500
HEIGHT

seen further west, but it makes up for it with its wildlife. Until recently there were few visitors to this land and large tracts of mountain country were left undisturbed. It is therefore the best area on the GR 10 to observe birds of prey. Eagles and vultures can be seen riding the thermals (to aid in their observation it may be worthwhile to carry a light pair of binoculars).

Saint-Jean-Pied-de-Port is a charming town and a good place to take a rest day. It is a medieval settlement on the banks of the River Nive and literally means 'at the foot of the gate'. The 'gate' is the crossing into Spain some 5 miles to the south, and the town is where so many pilgrims have rested before crossing the Pyrenees on their way into Spain. The symbol of their pilgrimage, the cockle shell of Santiago de Compostela, is in evidence all around the town. There are many ancient houses and churches to see and a museum detailing the medieval pilgrimages. During the summer a son et lumière is held and the annual fête features many attractions. However, during the fête (usually the first or second week in August) it is very difficult to obtain accommodation in Saint-Jean-Pied-de-Port.

Whilst walking through Basque country be sure to sample the delicious Basque food on offer. Gâteau Basque is to be recommended. Beware of imitations elsewhere!

SECTION 1: DAY 1

HENDAYE to OLHETTE

DISTANCE:	13½ miles	(21.7km)
ASCENT:	2463ft	(750m)
DESCENT:	2250ft	(685m)

	Timings					
	Sect.	Accum.	Shop	Bar/ Café	Restau- rant	Accomm- odation
HENDAYE			++	++	++	H+ CP
RN 10	1.15	1.15	-	-	-	-
BIRIATOU	1.00	2.15	-	-	++	H+
COL D'IBARDIN	1.50	4.05	++	+	+	-
VENTA D'INZOLA	1.00	5.05	+	+	-	-
OLHETTE	1.20	6.25	-	-	+	G

Hendaye has two main-line railway stations (SNCF): Hendaye Plage and Hendaye Ville.

The GR 10 begins officially at the casino on the sea front at Hendaye. Turn your back on the Atlantic and begin the long journey to the Mediterranean. Bear in mind the words of the Marquise du Deffand: "La distance n'y fait rien; il n'y a que le premier pas qui coûte." (The distance doesnt's matter; it's only the first step that is difficult.) In a few days/weeks/months you can decide whether you agree with him!

From the casino take the Boulevard du Général-Léclerc which leads to a small square where you turn right down the Rue des Citronniers. Turn left at the boulevard which follows the bay and continue for some distance, until about 50 yards before a bridge where you turn left to descend the Rue de Belcenia. Continue along the Rue Parcheteguia, pass under a railway line and follow the road out of Hendaye.

On a small hill overlooking the town the road bends to the right and descends. Take a tarmacked track on the left here. Initially some blue and white waymarks (signifying a local walk) are more obvious than the red and white GR 10 signs which occur rather spasmodically. The route is a little unclear in this area. However keep to the main track and eventually the blue and white signs veer to the right. The GR 10 continues to descend to join a tarmac track which leads to the main road.

Cross the Route National 10 and turn left. Bear right off the road and descend a small wooded path. Eventually you join a track which descends from a small ridge to pass under the motorway (autoroute A 63) by a corrugated iron tunnel. Turn right to climb up to a path and continue along this to emerge onto a road. Turn left into Biriatou.

Walk through this hamlet and look for the sign to the Col d'Ibardin. The path rises steeply and just below a small ridge you take the path on the right which meanders below the peaks, eventually crossing the Col d'Osin (1228ft;374m). From here you follow a wide grassy track gaining height. When the high point of the path is reached, descend to a large track which leads to a series of shops, cafés, restaurants and stalls just before the road at the Col d'Ibardin (1041ft;317m). This is a popular area for tourists from the coast.

Join the D 404 at the Col and turn left (north). After about 50 yards take the small path to the right of the road. Climb first towards the ridge before descending into a wooded valley by a stream. The route approaches the D 404 again but, about 100 yards before this road, you descend to the right into the wooded valley to follow streams to the Venta d'Inzola (a Spanish café, but prices are in French francs). This establishment also sells provisions.

From the Venta d'Inzola retrace your steps for about 20 yards to cross the river by a cement bridge. Follow the path as it gains height to emerge at the Col du Grand-Escargas (900ft;274m). An obvious path leads north from here to descend gradually to the hamlet of Olhette (213ft;65m). The gîte d'étape (good dinner and breakfast reported) will be found near to where the path turns right to cross the River Larroungo.

SECTION 1: DAY 2

OLHETTE to FERME ESTEBEN

DISTANCE:	20½ miles	(33km)
ASCENT:	3650ft	(1111m)
DESCENT:	1957ft	(596m)

	Timings Sect.	Accum.	Shop	Bar/ Café	Restau- rant	Accomm- odation
OLHETTE		-	-	+	G	
COL DES TROIS FONTAINES	1.15	1.15	-	-	-	C
SARE	1.30	2.45	++	++	++	H+ (CP)
AINHOA	2.45	5.30	++	++	++	H+ (CP)
CHAPELLE DE L'AUBEPINE	.40	6.10	-	-	-	-
COL DES TROIS CROIX	.50	7.00	-	-	-	-
FERME ESTEBEN	1.50	8.50	-	-	-	G

This is rather a long day, followed by an even harder one (see Day 3). The terrain is not exceptionally severe and so these two days can be managed without too much stress. However it would be possible to split Days 2 and 3 into three much shorter days, viz Olhette to Aïnhoa to Bidarray to Saint-Etienne-de-Baïgorry. Those inexperienced at long distance mountain walking, or tired after the first day's walk, should seriously consider dividing the route into these three shorter days.

Cross the River Larroungo and ascend the path on its right bank. The path soon leaves the river and continues climbing to reach the Col des Trois Fontaines (1849ft;563m). About 150 yards to the north (left) of the col is a very small, rather dirty cabane (sleeps about five people maximum). The area is suitable for wild camping with a good view back to the Atlantic and a water source nearby.

From the Col des Trois Fontaines the route passes through trees to reach a railway line near to a small railway station. The little mountain train runs to the summit of La Rhune. (This peak with its attendant radio mast will be visible for the next day or two.) Cross the railway track and follow the direction of the signpost to Sare. The descent down into the valley is a gentle one, passing several attractive farm buildings before emerging onto the road leading into Sare (pay particular attention during the latter stages of this descent and follow

Sare

the red/white markings carefully to avoid encountering the road to Sare too soon).

Sare (230ft;70m) is a typical small Basque town with several cafés, restaurants, hotels and tourists. There are two campsites in the neighbourhood, the nearest about three quarters of a mile from the village. It may be possible to get a bus from here to Saint-Jean-de-Luz. On entering Sare one will meet a signpost indicating two alternative routes for the GR 10 on the next stage of the journey. One of these is a relatively new ridge route which has not been tried by the author, but which may be preferable to the original walk to Aïnhoa, which is rather dull and involves some (albeit quiet) road walking. Reports suggest that this ridge route is now the standard route, but that like the old traditional route it is also rather dull, involving a considerable amount of road walking. (It passes three bars within the first hour from Sare.)

For the traditional route turn left at the sign indicating the two GR 10 alternatives and make for the village square. Follow the red/white flashes up from the square to pass a petrol station on the right. This route is partly on tarmac track and partly on ancient path, initially through a wooded valley, then a farming area and finally following a stream through superb ancient woodland before emerging on the

Calvary at the Chapelle de L'Aubépine

D 4. The ridge route joins the original GR 10 just before this road, but the two part company again immediately after crossing the D 4 (they finally meet up again at Aïnhoa). The original route is quite easy to follow; just walk along the D 4 in a north-westerly direction before taking a path on the right which climbs at first but soon levels out into a track which is then followed to Aïnhoa (394ft;120m).

Aïnhoa has a small church, pelota wall and several cafés, shops and hotels. There is a campsite about 1½ miles from the village.

Follow the D 20 past the church and shortly afterwards turn left down into a small street signposted 'Argi-Eder'. The road soon begins to climb quite steeply, passing several 'stations of the cross' on the ascent to the Chapelle de l'Aubépine (1281ft;390m). This is a good place for a rest in the shade of the trees surrounding the chapel. Continue to ascend, passing the impressive crucifixes (arranged as a calvary). The path skirts along the lower slopes of Ereby. At the first col (1609ft;490m) there is a source of drinking water from a water trough. (Note: the trough has been reported dry by some walkers and the nearby stream is of suspect origin.) The route turns towards the south and climbs to the Col des Trois Croix (1675ft;510m). Oddly enough there are no crosses here.

Continue upwards on the main track for a little while before taking a small path to the left (easy to miss). This rejoins the main track before dropping down to a col. Keep to the main track to regain height at the Col Zuccuta (1859ft;566m). This col is not named on the 1:50,000 IGN map, but is marked as a height of 566. The path crosses the col and then flanks Mont Bizkayluze to arrive at Ferme Esteben (1905ft;580m) where there is a gîte d'étape.

SECTION 1: DAY 3

FERME ESTEBEN to SAINT-ETIENNE-DE-BAIGORRY

DISTANCE:	17 miles	(27.4km)
ASCENT:	4537ft	(1381m)
DESCENT:	5909ft	(1799m)

	Timings					
	Sect.	Accum.	Shop	Bar/ Café	Restau- rant	Accomm- odation
FERME ESTEBEN			-	-	-	G
COL DE MEHATCHE	.45	.45	-	-	-	-
BIDARRAY	2.30	3.15	+	+	+	G. H+
PIC D'IPARLA	2.30	5.45	-	-	-	-
COL D'HARRIETA	1.15	7.00	-	-	-	-
COL DE BUZTANZELHAY	1.20	8.20	-	-	-	-
SAINT-ETIÉNNE-DE-BAIGORRY	2.00	10.20	++	++	++	G. H+. CP

Bidarray has a railway station (SNCF). There is a SNCF tourist bus from Saint-Etienne-de-Baïgorry to Bayonne and also to Saint-Jean-Pied-de-Port. Saint-Etienne-de-Baïgorry has a tourist office.

The ridge route from Bidarray to the Col de Buztanzelhay offers little or no possibility of water. This is a long and fairly demanding section.

Follow the road out of the farmyard to the Col des Veaux (1773ft; 540m). For the next few miles the GR 10 is very close to the Spanish border. The path soon veers away to the right from the road and begins the climb to the Col de Méhatche where the route once again joins the road. The view ahead now appears quite mountainous; the coastal foothills are being left behind. The GR 10 soon takes a grassy path heading towards the south-east. About 100 yards before a bergerie the path descends steeply into a ravine (watch carefully for the red/white flashes). The path initially descends in a south-westerly direction but soon turns to descend towards the east. The descent is sometimes rough underfoot and care is necessary. Some walkers find this section particularly difficult. The path skirts the hillside losing height until just before a farm it picks up an old stony footpath to emerge onto a road. Continue on this road for over a mile until just before a bridge over the River Bastan, then take a path on the right climbing up through the trees. Join the road once again and walk into the centre of Bidarray (493ft;150m) where there is a fronton, a church, a gîte d'étape and a variety of other facilities.

Retrace the route to the edge of the village and turn left to climb up a small waymarked road. Follow the red/white signs to pick up a track which rises steeply to gain the Col Pagalepoa at 1478ft (450m). A small bergerie is located here. The well marked path continues to rise in a south-easterly direction, passing a ruined bergerie at 2388ft (727m). Follow the ridge for several miles with a sharp drop down into France on the left and a gentler decline towards Spain over to the right. Eventually reach the summit of Pic d'Iparla (3429ft;1044m) which is marked by a white Spanish concrete plinth. There is an extensive view from here.

Continue to follow the ridge which forms the Franco-Spanish border in a south-westerly direction to climb two small peaks (at 3422ft;1042m and at 3340ft;1017m) before descending to the Col de Gapelu (3104ft;945m). Ascend the Pic de Toutoulia (3228ft;983m) and descend to the wooded Col d'Harrieta (2654ft;808m). There is a footpath down to the village of Urdos from here (restaurant).

The GR 10, however, keeps to the ridge heading generally in a southerly direction. The path rises through woodland, soon reaching L'Astaté (3356ft;1022m) then dropping to another col at 3153ft (960m) before climbing to yet another high point, the Pic de Buztanzelhay (3376ft;1028m). Descend next to the col of the same name where the GR 10 leaves the Franco-Spanish border and descends the valley to the east. Walk alongside a small stream and reach a large solitary tree where there is a good source of water (the only water between Bidarray and Saint-Etienne-de-Baïgorry).

The path now descends a little before rising again to another ridge. This is a good area to spot vultures. Follow a track downhill, then a footpath and finally a green track to emerge on a small road by the fronton of Saint-Etienne-de-Baïgorry (532ft;162m). Here will be found many facilities, including a bank. The gîte d'étape is about 0.6 miles (1km) from the town on a waymarked path. There is a hotel nearby which provides good food.

SECTION 1: DAY 4

SAINT-ETIENNE-DE-BAIGORRY to SAINT-JEAN-PIED-DE-PORT

DISTANCE:	$10^{1/2}$ miles	(17km)
ASCENT:	2847ft	(867m)
DESCENT:	2864ft	(872m)

	Timings Sect.	Accum.	Shop	Bar/ Café	Restau- rant	Accomm- odation
SAINT-ETIENNE-DE-BAIGORRY			++	++	++	G. H+. CP
COL D'AHARZA	2.00	2.00	-	-	-	-
COL D'URDANZIA	.50	2.50	-	-	-	-
MONHOA	.30	3.20	-	-	-	-
LASSE	2.15	5.35	-	+	-	-
SAINT-JEAN-PIED-DE-PORT	.40	6.15	++	++	++	G. H+. CP

Saint-Jean-Pied-de-Port has numerous facilities including supermarkets, banks, a tourist office and a railway station (SNCF) for trains to Bayonne. There are also a number of local coach services. Saint-Jean-Pied-de-Port is one of the largest towns on the GR 10.

After the efforts of the last few days, this stage is relatively short and not too strenuous. The non-purists could even take a bus ride down the valley from Saint-Etienne to Saint-Jean-Pied-de-Port!

Leave Saint-Etienne-de-Baïgorry near to the gendarmerie. Turn left up a small street and pass under the railway line. Turn right and follow the road uphill. Join a track and follow the red/white signs as the route climbs around the mountain of Oylarandoy, passing several ruined bergeries before finally climbing to the Col d'Aharza (2411ft;734m). From here the GR 10 continues to climb before dropping

River, St-Etienne-de-Baïgorry

to the Col de Leizarze (2719ft;828m). After this the path rises again, first in a south-easterly direction, then slowly bearing east to descend to the Col d'Urdanzia (2854ft;869m). This can be identified by the presence of an iron cross.

Climb the ridge in a north-easterly direction to attain the summit of Monhoa (3353ft;1021m) from where there are extensive views down into the Saint-Jean-Pied-de-Port valley. Leave the summit in an easterly direction to drop to the 2463ft (750m) level where there are two water troughs. Leave the ridge here and descend, at first towards the north-west. A well waymarked track descends gradually to become an asphalted track which emerges at the church and fronton of the small village of Lasse.

Walk down the road in the direction of Saint-Jean-Pied-de-Port. After a little over half a mile cross the River Nive d'Arnéguy and continue to enter the bustling town of Saint-Jean-Pied-de-Port (516ft;157m). There are several hotels in the town (Hotel Itzalpea can be recommended) and a gîte d'étape at 9 Route d'Uhart in the house of Joseph Etchegoin who also has rooms.

Saint-Jean-Pied-de-Port is an important staging post for those pilgrims walking from Le Puy, or other destinations in France, to Santiago de Compostela in north-western Spain.

SECTION 1: DAY 5

SAINT-JEAN-PIED-DE-PORT to BEHEROBIE

DISTANCE:	$11^{1/2}$ miles	(18.5km)
ASCENT:	3097ft	(943m)
DESCENT:	2529ft	(770m)

	Timings Sect.	Accum.	Shop	Bar/ Café	Restau-rant	Accomm-odation
SAINT-JEAN-PIED-DE-PORT			++	++	++	G H+. CP
HONTO	1.30	1.30	-	-	-	-
VIERGE D'ORISSON	1.35	3.05	-	-	-	-
BEHEROBIE	2.10	5.15	-	+	+	H

The route to Chalet Pedro via Béhérobie, as described below, although still feasible, has now been abandoned by the French Long Distance Footpath Authorities as the GR 10. The trail now leaves Saint-Jean on the D 401 and then passes Caro, Estérencuby, Phagalcette, Iraukotuturry and the Sommet d'Occabé to reach Chalet Pedro. This route is clearly marked on the current IGN maps as the GR 10 and is waymarked on the ground with the usual red and white waymarks. For those following this new section of GR 10 there is a new gîte d'étape at Estérencuby (opened in July, 1995) which is very modern, clean and recommended. It is owned and run by the hotel on the west side of the river. There is a second hotel in Estérencuby as well as a couple of bars. It is possible for very fit walkers to walk from Saint-Jean-Pied-de-Port to Col Bagarguiac in one day, but this makes for a very long stage. It is preferable to break the journey at Estérencuby which is circa 3-4 hours walking from Saint Jean. The next stage from Estérencuby to Col Bagarguiac is circa 8 hours (note that some walkers have reported navigational difficulties on the section of this trail after Occabé, so that diligence is required).

At Saint-Jean-Pied-de-Port the GR 10 meets with the GR 65. The latter is the ancient route of pilgrimage to Santiago de Compostela in Spain. The two routes cross each other several times during the ascent from the town and are co-incident for the last half mile or so to the Vierge d'Orisson. Here the GR 65 takes the road into Spain whilst the

GR 10 descends to the valley of the Nive.

Leave Saint-Jean-Pied-de-Port by the Porte d'Espagne heading in a south-westerly direction. Pass the gendarmerie and turn right down the Rue de Mayorga. Follow the GR 10 signs to walk up a small road between two walls. This later becomes a track and then a path. Continue in a southerly direction eventually climbing onto a ridge to pass a bergerie and a TV relay station. The track emerges at a road to meet the GR 65 above the hamlet of Honto.

Turn right at the road but after only 30 yards or so turn right off this road onto a pleasant grassy track. This level path hugs the hillside, eventually crossing a stream and climbing one of its banks. The path then climbs very steeply through woods (usually this is quite wet and slippery). The GR 10 leaves this wooded area at a bergerie. The path climbs another ridge and then reaches the road again to rejoin the GR 65 once more. The GR 10 and GR 65 both ascend the road for over half a mile to reach the statue of the virgin - the Vierge d'Orisson (3613ft;1100m). From this madonna there are extensive views, but there is also a car park and usually plenty of tourists.

Here the GR 10 leaves the GR 65 and passes to the right of the statue taking a wide track which descends at first in a southerly direction, but which soon veers to the east. Care is needed after about 1¼ miles (2km) to avoid missing the red/white waymarked small path to the right of the main track. This path descends a grassy slope towards the Cabanes d'Asquéta. Follow the path as it leads to an old field boundary where the GR 10 turns down to the right (take care to follow the red/white waymarks carefully in this area to avoid losing the route). Descend and follow the route to the left to pick up an old footpath which leads down into the Nive valley. On this descent pass two bergeries where a farm track is joined. Continue downhill on this track to pass two other farmhouses (the first of which usually sells cheese). At the second house the track goes through the courtyard marked 'Privée' (if walking the GR 10, passage is permitted). The grass track finally emerges at the car park of the Hotel de la Nive at Béhérobie (1084ft;330m). There are possibilities for wild camping in the area (with plenty of water available) but permission from the farmers/landowners should first be obtained.

SECTION 1: DAY 6

BEHEROBIE to COL BAGARGUIAC

DISTANCE:	14½ miles	(23.7km)
ASCENT:	6046ft	(1841m)
DESCENT:	2772ft	(844m)

	Timings					
	Sect.	Accum.	Shop	Bar/ Café	Restau-rant	Accomm-odation
BEHEROBIE			-	+	+	H
COL D'ERROZATE	2.00	2.00	-	-	-	-
CHALET PEDRO	3.40	5.40	-	+	+	-
COL BAGARGUIAC	1.50	7.30	+	+	+	G. CP

A pleasant stage in the heart of Basque hill country.

About 60 yards north of the hotel take a path off the road climbing gently towards the south and passing a farm on the right. Shortly afterwards cross a stream by a small bridge and ascend the valley through woodland. At the 700m mark the path levels for a while through pasture before climbing again to reach the Col d'Errozate (3534ft;1076m) at the Franco-Spanish border.

Continue to ascend in a north-north-easterly direction over grass on an unmarked path to reach a dirt track which passes underneath the summit of Errozate. This track continues to cross the summit of Aranoheguy (4246ft;1293m). The path leaves this track to zig-zag down a grassy slope to cross the marshy ground of the Cuvette Marécageuse d'Irau. The route can be somewhat confusing here, but follow the red/ white waymarks and the map carefully to cross a small stream and climb once more. The walk can be quite strenuous in the heat of the day as there is little shade. Eventually pass the rock strewn summit d'Occabé (4782ft;1456m). Begin the descent still on open hillside at first, but soon entering woodland where a good path meanders downhill to a surfaced road at the Chalet Pedro (3251ft;990m). This restaurant provides very good food and is popular with tourists. There is no accommodation here, but across the road from the restaurant by a stream is a pleasant spot for wild camping.

From Chalet Pedro continue northwards along the road (another café) for over half a mile, passing an artificial lake. Leave the road for a path on the right which climbs through woodland. After a while this descends to a road by another artificial lake. Cross the road and a bridge over the lake to re-enter woodland and climb up to the Col Bagarguiac (4358ft;1327m). There is a large tourist complex here (Forêt d'Iraty) consisting of three artificial lakes, a shop, café, restaurant and many wooden chalets or holiday homes. There is a gîte d'étape and a campsite.

SECTION 1: DAY 7

COL BAGARGUIAC to LOGIBAR

DISTANCE:	Route 1 - 6½ miles	(10.5km).
ASCENT:	Route 1 - 397ft	(121m).
DESCENT:	Route 1 - 3524ft	(1073m).
DISTANCE:	Route 2 - 10 miles	(16.1km)
ASCENT:	Route 2 - 1103ft	(336m)
DESCENT:	Route 2 - 4230ft	(1288m)

	Timings Sect.	Accum.	Shop	Bar/ Café	Restau-rant	Accomm-odation
Route 1						
COL BAGARGUIAC			+	+	+	G. CP
FORGES DE LARRAU	2.00	2.00	-	-	-	-
LARRAU	1.10	3.10	+	+	+	H+. CP
LOGIBAR	.45	3.55	-	-	+	G. H.
Route 2						
COL BAGARGUIAC			+	+	+	G. CP
CAYOLAR MENDIKOTZIAGUE	3.00	3.00	-	-	-	-
LOGIBAR	2.30	5.30	-	-	+	G. H.

There are two alternative routes for the GR 10 from Col Bagarguiac to Logibar. The shorter route visits the village of Larrau where there are shops, hotels and restaurants, and then descends on the road to Logibar.

The alternative route keeps to the mountains and involves more ascent and descent, but offers better scenery. Neither route is particularly long nor arduous, with far more descent than ascent, and the stage is really only a half-day's walk. In bad weather Route 1 is safer.

Route 1

Descend the road from the tourist complex in an easterly direction. After about 10 minutes, at the Col d'Orgambidesca (4217ft;1284m), turn right off the road and descend steeply towards the south-east, joining the road again some way further down. Stay on the road for a further 10 minutes to leave it on the left. Go over a small col and keep to a stony track to descend steeply. After about 50 minutes reach the road once again and turn left. A little further on leave the road again on the left just before it rises. Follow the red/white waymarks on a cross-country route, finally climbing quite steeply to emerge in the village of Larrau. Continue down the road in an easterly direction for just over 2 miles to the gîte d'étape on the right-hand side of the road at Logibar. (The restaurant adjacent to the gîte is highly recommended.)

Route 2

Take a woodland path which starts near the tennis courts. This descends in a northerly direction to the Col Iratzabaleta. Continue to climb and cross a ridge of the Pic des Escaliers and then descend to the north-east on a steep path. At 4105ft (1250m) meet a road. Follow this to the Crête Ugatzé (3842ft;1170m), leaving the road here to follow the ridge eastwards to Col Ugatzé (3760ft;1145m) and on to a lower col at 3514ft (1070m). Descend towards the south-east to the Cayolar Mendikotziague (3218ft;980m).

Leave the path and descend to a water trough, taking care to follow the waymarks through an area of boulders. A clear path descends south-south-east. Follow this until reaching a line of trees where a gently rising path is followed to cross a rocky area heading south-east. A track is joined which climbs to a col at 3340ft (1017m). Follow a ridge path towards the south-west for over 500 yards before veering to the right and descending on a path. Continue on an undulating path, crossing two further cols to arrive eventually at two farm buildings. Take a good path heading north-east, pass a water trough and continue down to a house where the path divides. Take the right branch descending to the south. Leave and short-cut this track on two occasions, eventually emerging at the D 26 road at Logibar (1232ft;375m) opposite the gîte d'étape.

SECTION 1: DAY 8

LOGIBAR to SAINTE-ENGRACE

DISTANCE:	16 miles	(25.8km)
ASCENT:	3672ft	(1118m)
DESCENT:	2834ft	(863m)

	Timings Sect.	Accum.	Shop	Bar/ Café	Restau-rant	Accomm-odation
LOGIBAR			-	-	+	G. H.
PASSERELLE D'HOLZARTE	.35	.35	-	-	-	-
PONT D'OLHADUBI	.55	1.30	-	-	-	-
COL D'ANHAOU	2.20	3.50	-	-	-	-
GORGES DE KAKOUETA (entrance)	2.30	6.20	-	+	-	-
HONDAGNEU	.30	6.50	-	-	+	H
SAINTE-ENGRACE	.20	7.10	-	+	+	G

Note that the Pont d'Olhadubi was swept away by a storm in June 1992, which also caused sufficient damage to force the closure of the Gorges de Kakouéta. The route of the GR 10 has been modified as a consequence and the walker must follow the new route as indicated by the waymarks and with due reference to the latest IGN map.

This is a superb section, skirting two impressive steep-sided limestone gorges before dropping down into the Sainte-Engrâce valley. This beautiful valley is the home of the ancient Basque commune of Santazi, whose settlements are to be seen scattered along the surrounding hillsides.

The Gorges de Kakouéta (if now open) are well worth a visit (allow half a day). There is a small entrance fee and tickets are on sale in the nearby refreshment bar. The gorges are popular with tourists and there are wooden walkways taking the visitor right into the heart of the very deep, steep-sided gorge, passing waterfalls and limestone formations. The gorge is refreshingly cool during the heat of the summer.

From the gîte d'étape at Logibar follow the footpath signposted to the Gorges d'Holzarté. Climb on this path with the river on the right to a suspension bridge (the Passerelle d'Holzarté, built in 1922). Walk over this bridge and continue on the opposite bank of the river, at first

Church at Sainte-Engrâce

climbing and then on a level path. Reach a small bridge over the river on the left. Cross this and continue to climb, this time in a northerly direction. The route climbs and eventually turns to resume a south-easterly direction. The GR 10 reaches a dirt road which is followed for over a mile. Leave this track on the left where indicated by the red/ white waymarks and climb steeply to the Col d'Anhaou (4542ft;1383m). This ridge divides the two Basque communes of Larrau and Sainte-Engrâce (Santazi).

From the col follow the dirt track, later keeping the limestone Gorge of Kakouéta on the right. This area is somewhat confusing to negotiate because of the presence of several relatively new, bull-dozed dirt roads which have obliterated some of the route. Further down in the valley a road will be reached. Follow this for a short way before turning right to descend a steep stony track to the road at the entrance to the Gorges de Kakouéta.

Follow this road (the D 113) in an easterly direction, climbing gradually up the valley. After about 1¼ miles (2km) pass the Hotel-Restaurant of Hondagneu on the right and continue up the valley to reach the picturesque 11th century church of Sainte-Engrâce (2069ft;630m) on the right-hand side of the road at Senta. A café and the gîte d'étape are opposite the church.

INTRODUCTION

Béarn is an ancient division of the Pyrenees and was once one of the largest of the several independent states in these mountains. Pays Basque and Béarn are now both contained in the modern département of the Pyrénées-Atlantiques, but the two regions are still culturally, architecturally and topographically distinct. After leaving the Basque country the GR 10 enters the high mountains of Béarn, an area dominated by the valleys of the Aspe and Ossau and containing several of the most shapely and impressive of the Pyrenean mountains.

The route climbs steeply and unrelentingly from Sainte-Engrâce to reach the Col de la Pierre Saint Martin on the border with Spain before descending to the modern ski resort of Arette-Pierre-Saint-Martin, an ugly development of high-rise concrete apartment blocks. An area of scattered and broken limestone (arres) is now reached. A number of pot-holes (gouffres) will be seen which allow speleologists access to an extensive cave system beneath the surface.

The route continues to the village of Lescun in a high pastoral valley ringed by a great arc of mountains, the most prominent of which is the pyramidal shaped Pic d'Anie at 8224ft (2504m), the most westerly of the major Pyrenean summits. The area also marks the western end of the Pyrenean National Park which runs from here to the Néouvielle massif some 60 miles to the east. The area of the Park is some 45,700 hectares, but it is highly irregular in shape and is never more than about 8 miles in width.

Wolves only became extinct in Béarn in the 1930's and these mountains are the last remaining stronghold in western Europe of the brown bear. There are probably less than twenty bears remaining in the Pyrenees and there is very little chance of sighting one of these animals, although shepherds in the Lescun area often recount tales of sheep killings attributed to bears.

The GR 10 crosses over from the Aspe valley to Bious-Artigues in the valley of the Ossau via the Col d'Ayous, the first time that an altitude over 2000m, (6568ft) has been reached. Use is made of the Chemin de la Mâture, a path deeply cut into the side of a cliff and said to have been built by convicts and designed by naval engineers two centuries ago. It was used to transport felled pine trees destined for

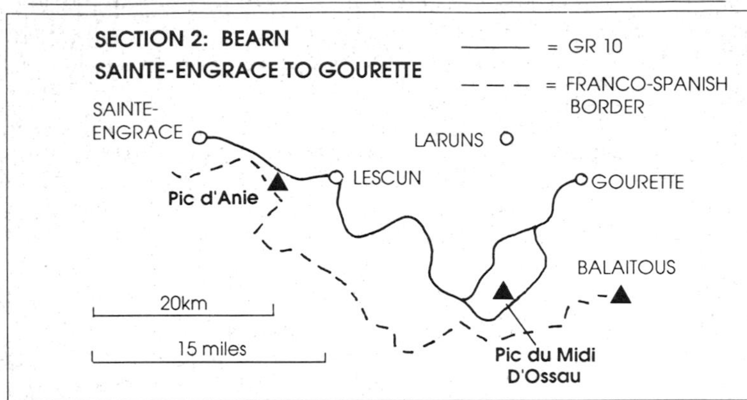

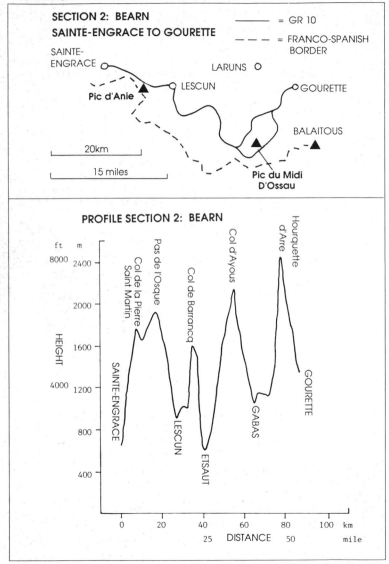

PROFILE SECTION 2: BEARN

ft m
8000 2400
2000
1600
4000 1200
800
400
HEIGHT

SAINTE-ENGRACE
Col de la Pierre Saint Martin
Pas de l'Osque
LESCUN
Col de Barrancq
ETSAUT
Col d'Ayous
GABAS
Hourquette d'Arre
GOURETTE

0 20 40 60 80 100 km
25 DISTANCE 50 mile

The Col de Suzon seen from the 'tourist route' of ascent of the Pic du Midi d'Ossau

Tourist route, Pic du Midi d'Ossau

the naval dockyards of Bayonne for conversion into the tall masts of sailing ships.

Much has been written concerning the shapely Pic du Midi d'Ossau whose characteristic silhouette has adorned the pages of many climbing and walking books and magazines. Although not of any great height, this twin-peaked mountain stands alone and its massive granite walls can be recognised for many miles around. The Grand and Petit Pic are separated by a deep cleft known as La Fourche which renders the mountain highly photogenic. The Pic du Midi d'Ossau should be viewed from all angles and at all times of the day; the circuit of the peak described in the text is highly recommended.

Leaving the Ossau valley at Gabas, the GR 10 crosses the steep and sometimes snow covered Hourquette d'Arre to reach the ski village of Gourette. The region has several sulphurous thermal springs around which spa towns have developed with names like Eaux-Bonnes (good waters) and Eaux-Chaudes (hot waters). Numerous other spa towns will be visited on the journey eastwards through the Pyrenees. They have been attracting people afflicted with an assortment of ailments for several centuries. Note the distinctive design of the buildings in these and other towns and villages in Béarn, particularly the shape of the roofs and the use of grey slates which replace the tiles characteristic of the Basque region.

If leaving or joining the GR 10 in Béarn, the regional capital and university town of Pau should be visited. It had a strong British presence in the last century and today is a bustling town and a good place to stock-up on maps, guidebooks and posters of the Pyrenees. The château (birthplace of Henry IV of France) is worth a visit and, before leaving, take time to stand in the Boulevard des Pyrénées and look across the plain to the mountains in the south. Here is one of the finest of the long-range views of the Pyrenees and it is possible to pick out your favourite peaks in the 60-mile arc of the western Pyrenees visible.

Pau is linked to Oloron-Sainte-Marie where the Gave d'Aspe and Gave d'Ossau meet. This town with its two large, ornate churches is also well worth a visit if time is still available for excursions.

SECTION 2: DAY 1

SAINTE-ENGRACE to ARETTE-PIERRE-SAINT-MARTIN

DISTANCE:	$6^{1}/_{2}$ miles	(10·5km)
ASCENT:	3842ft	(1170m)
DESCENT:	525ft	(160m)

	Timings Sect.	Accum.	Shop	Bar/ Café	Restau-rant	Accomm-odation
SAINTE-ENGRACE			-	+	+	G
CABANE DU COUP	3.00	3.00	-	-	-	-
COL DE LA PIERRE SAINT MARTIN	.50	3.50	-	-	-	-
ARETTE-PIERRE-SAINT MARTIN	.45	4.35	++	++	++	G. H+

Although this is a relatively short day, the GR 10 is for the first time entering really big mountain country and there is a lot of steep climbing. It is possible to combine this stage with tomorrow's itinerary to Lescun, but this would make a long, hard day requiring a very early start.

Leave the gîte d'étape at Sainte-Engrâce and turn left to descend the road. Follow the red / white signs to a small bridge. Cross the road and ascend on a waymarked footpath. Soon enter a small ravine (Ravin d'Arpidia). Here, crossing from the commune of Sainte-Engrâce into Arette, the walker is entering Béarn, leaving the Basque country behind.

Ascend very steeply through dense woodland (which provides ample shade on a hot day). Some of the red / white markers are difficult to follow in places as the route has been obliterated in part by a relatively new dirt track ascending through the trees. (It has been reported that the waymarking has been improved and that the route is now easy to follow.) However, the way is always upwards and just before emerging from the trees a large and elaborately sculptured and painted water trough should be passed. Shortly after leaving the tree line you pass a ruined bergerie (Cabane d'Escuret de Bas) at 4351ft (1325m). Continue to climb steeply until passing above and to the left of a large bergerie at 4998ft (1522m). This is the Cabane du Coup. There is still some climbing from here but on easy, wide angled zig-zags until the ridge ahead is reached at the Col de la Pierre Saint Martin (5780ft;1760m). Here at the frontier with Spain there is a spectacular view of high mountains dominated by the magestic Pic d'Anie (8224ft;2504m). The Col de la Pierre Saint Martin is the site of an ancient ceremony dating back to 1375 between the people of Barétous in Béarn and Ronçal in Navarre, Spain. Every 13th July the ceremony between the two communities takes place to re-establish their ancient grazing rights.

Descend to the road (built in 1973), turn left and after just under a mile, where the road bends to the left, continue straight on to pass under the ski-lift cables. Follow the red/white flashes to descend to the ski-complex of Arette-Pierre-Saint-Martin (5386ft;1640m) where there is a gîte d'étape. Arette-Pierre-Saint-Martin is a monstrous concrete complex, totally out of sympathy with its surroundings. Chalets and multi-story hotels abound. Flee it as soon as possible!

Arette-Pierre-Saint-Martin is also the starting point for the three day excursion called Tour de la Vallée de Barétous which is marked on the 1:50,000 IGN map.

SECTION 2: DAY 2

ARETTE-PIERRE-SAINT-MARTIN to LESCUN

DISTANCE:	9 miles	(14.5km)
ASCENT:	1189ft	(362m)
DESCENT:	2962ft	(902m)

	Timings Sect.	Accum.	Shop	Bar/ Café	Restau-rant	Accomm-odation
ARETTE-PIERRE-SAINT-MARTIN			++	++	++	G. H+
PAS DE L'OSQUE	2.50	2.50	-	-	-	-
PAS D'AZUNS	.25	3.15	-	-	-	-
REFUGE DE LABEROUAT	1.20	4.35	-	-	-	R
GITE D'ETAPE (LESCUN)	.25	5.00	-	-	-	*G

* Meals are not usually available at the gîte as the warden lives in Lescun. There are shops and a hotel-restaurant down in the village. It is a 30-minute walk down to Lescun, but considerably longer on the climb back up to the gîte!

From the Pas d'Azuns. The first view of the Pic du Midi d'Ossau

Take a prominent dirt road heading south from the ski-resort. Follow this as it changes direction several times before leaving it to head eastwards, passing under the cable of a chair lift to arrive at a large limestone plateau, the Arres de Camlong. Note that from here a waymarked path can be taken to the summit of Pic d'Anie (8224ft;2504m). Start at the marked rock (Pic d'Anie) and follow the arrows. For the GR 10 follow the red/white waymarks carefully to traverse a dry, rocky area generally in an easterly direction. The route is mostly on a good narrow path, but this is lost in places and so care is required to maintain direction. The area is fully exposed to the sun; the heat coupled with glare from the limestone rocks can make this an inhospitable place. The only shade available is that provided by a few scattered pine trees, so make sure that plenty of water is carried. The route is somewhat undulating but eventually makes a steep but short ascent to a col, the Pas de l'Osque (6312ft;1922m). [Some walkers have reported difficulty in following the correct line of the GR 10 on the route to the Pas de l'Osque. If the waymarks are mislaid the tendency is to veer downhill (north). It is important to keep close under the rock face on the right(south).] This has a prominent rocky tower to its left. From here the next objective can be seen (the Pas d'Azuns, 6151ft;1873m). Descend and reascend on an obvious path to this col.

From here there is an extensive view down into the Vallée d'Aspe and of the nearby peaks (Pic du Soumcouy and the Pic d'Anie). Look also to the far horizon for the first view of the Pic du Midi d'Ossau; its characteristic shape will be observed for several days to come.

Descend from the Pas d'Azuns to the cabanes of the Cap de la Baitch (5547ft;1689m) where there is a good source of water. From here there is also another footpath leading to the summit of the Pic d'Anie. From the cabanes take the clear path descending down the left side of the valley. Pass through pleasant woodland and, on leaving this, reach a large refuge (the Refuge de Labérouat) at 4736ft (1442m). Take the road from here descending for about 25 minutes until a sign indicating the gîte d'étape is reached. This is 100 yards or so off the road on the left (and uphill a little!). Note that there is now also a gîte d'étape in Lescun itself - it is situated directly opposite the Hotel Pic d'Anie (which owns it).

SECTION 2: DAY 3

LESCUN to BORCE

DISTANCE:	9 miles	(14.5km)
ASCENT:	2670ft	(813m)
DESCENT:	4148ft	(1263m)

	Timings Sect.	Accum.	Shop	Bar/ Café	Restau- rant	Accomm- odation
GITE D'ETAPE (LESCUN)			-	-	-	G
LESCUN	.30	.30	+	+	+	G H
FERME LESTREMEAU	.55	1.25	-	-	-	-
LHERS	.50	2.15	-	-	-	G
COL DE BARRANCQ	1.50	4.05	-	-	-	-
BORCE	2.15	6.20	+	+	+	G. (CP)

The gîte d'étape at Lescun is also the starting point for another walking excursion, called the Tour de la Vallée d'Aspe which is marked on the 1:50,000 IGN map.

From the gîte walk back down the path to the road where you turn left to continue the descent into Lescun (2956ft;900m). This most

Borce

picturesque of villages is surrounded by a cirque of mountains dominated by Pic d'Anie. There is a shop and the Hotel du Pic d'Anie is in the centre of the village.

Follow the red / white signs from the small war memorial, through the village and down the road to reach and cross the Pont Moulin. Continue following the waymarks up various narrow and sometimes overgrown paths and tracks to Ferme Lestremeau. Cheese is usually on sale here and water may be available. From here it is a more or less level walk, sometimes through woodland, to the widely spread group of farms known as Lhers (3274ft;997m). Take to the small road but after a while leave it on the right to follow the waymarks steeply uphill. The views in this region of the Cirque de Lescun are extremely good. Soon enter trees and then follow a track, taking the waymarked short-cuts, to climb uphill until unexpectedly reaching the summit (Col de Barrancq, 5258ft;1601m). This is one of the few cols on the GR 10 where there is no view as it is covered by dense woodland.

Follow a winding path down through the trees to emerge at a ruined cottage (Cabane d'Udapet-de-Haut, 4975ft;1515m). Head down the mountainside soon passing another small cabane. Walk through an area of ferns, pass a stream and continue downhill until eventually meeting the road above the typically Béarnais village of Borce

(2135ft;650m). For the campsite turn right here and walk for a further half mile uphill (good showers and a day-room). For Borce and the gîte d'étape take the track down to the centre of the village. Borce has a fine church and also a grocer's and fruit shop, but no restaurant.

SECTION 2: DAY 4

BORCE to LAC DE BIOUS-ARTIGUES

DISTANCE:	13 miles	(21km)
ASCENT:	5215ft	(1588m)
DESCENT:	2696ft	(821m)

	Timings Sect.	Accum.	Shop	Bar/ Café	Restau- rant	Accomm- odation
BORCE			+	+	+	G (CP)
ETSAUT	.20	.20	++	++	++	G. H+
HOURQUETTE DE LARRY	4.45	5.05	-	-	-	-
COL D'AYOUS	.20	5.25	-	-	-	-
LACS D'AYOUS	.30	5.55	-	-	-	R
PLAINE DE BIOUS	.55	6.50	-	-	-	-
LAC DE BIOUS-ARTIGUES	.40	7.30	(+)*	-	-	R.(CP)*

* The campsite is about a mile from the Lac de Bious-Artigues along the D 231. The shop is situated on the campsite.

From Borce take the main road (N 134) down to the Aspe valley, cross the Gave d'Aspe and turn right to enter Etsaut. (Note: a new waymarked route, avoiding the road, has now been provided. It is signposted and crosses a new footbridge over the river.)This large village has several cafés, restaurants, a gîte d'étape, hotels and a National Park Information Centre. Pass through Etsaut remaining on the main road for just over a mile, then take a waymarked footpath leading off to the left. (To omit Etsaut it is possible to take a minor road from Borce and cross over the river by a bridge near to the area where the footpath mentioned above leaves the main road.) The footpath soon climbs and becomes a well defined stony track clinging to the mountainside. This is the Chemin de la Mâture. This track, which has an impressive drop on the right-hand side, climbs steeply, eventually reaching the Plateau de la Baigt de Saint-Cours at 3613ft (1100m) where there is a bergerie (water supply here). Continue on a well defined footpath, sometimes level, sometimes climbing and occasionally passing through woodland (note: refreshments are available en route at a small farmhouse, Borde de Passette, situated at a height of about 1200m), to reach the boundary of the Pyrenean National Park after about 1½ hours from the road. This is at the Cabane de la Baight de Saint-Cours (5123ft;1560m).

There is a steady ascent from here at first, but eventually the gradient steepens as the path zig-zags upwards. The path is well defined all the way to the Hourquette de Larry which bears a wooden signpost. This is at an altitude of 6749ft (2055m), the first time the GR 10 has passed the 2000m mark. Continue the ascent to the left on a good path to reach the Col d'Ayous (7176ft;2185m) which also sports a Pyrenean National Park wooden signpost. A short excursion to the Pic d'Ayous (7514ft;2288m) could be made from here.

From the Col d'Ayous follow an eroded path down through a series of zig-zags (there may be snowfields here) to Lac Gentau (6394ft;1947m) the first of the Lacs d'Ayous. This lake gives a superb reflection of the Pic du Midi d'Ossau. The Refuge d'Ayous (a National Park Refuge) is some 300 yards to the west on a rise above the lake. Continue on down past two other lakes (Lac du Mey and Lac Roumassot) passing through woodland on an ever widening and eroded path. Reach the Plaine de Bious and gradually descend to the artificial Lac de Bious-Artigues (4654ft;1417m). Walk along the shore of the lake to its far end to the Chalet du Club Pyrénéa Sports, situated just before the roadhead. It is necessary to join this organisation in order to book overnight accommodation. Membership can be obtained on the spot for a very small fee and this also entitles the member to stay at the Club Pyrénéa refuge in Gourette. If using a tent then walk down the D 231 for about a mile on the GR 10 route until a campsite is reached on the right-hand side of the road.

SECTION 2: EXCURSION

TOUR du PIC du MIDI D'OSSAU

DISTANCE:	$9^{1}/_{2}$ miles	(15.3km)
ASCENT:	2867ft	(873m)
DESCENT:	2867ft	(873m)

	Timings Sect.	Accum.	Shop	Bar/ Café	Restau- rant	Accomm- odation
CHALET DU CLUB PYRENEA SPORTS			(+)	-*	-*	R. (CP)
PLAINE DE BIOUS	.50	.50	-	-	-	-
LAC DE PEYREGET	1.25	2.15	-	-	-	-
LAC DE POMBIE	1.30	3.45	-	-*	-*	R
COL DE SUZON	.45	4.30	-	-	-	-
CHALET DU CLUB PYRENEA SPORTS	2.15	6.45	(+)	-*	-*	R. (CP)

* Both refuges offer refreshments and evening meals.

The Tour du Pic du Midi d'Ossau is one of the classic circular tours in the French Pyrenees and should not be missed by visitors to the area. It allows a close-up view of this superb peak from all sides and provides mountain scenery of the highest quality.

The Tour can of course be walked either way round, but it is described here in the traditional anti-clockwise direction. The walk fits nicely into a day without rushing and only a day sack need be carried. Therefore consider it a rest day; relax and enjoy the superb scenery. Alternatively the first half of the Tour to the Pombie hut could be made from the Plaine de Bious, on the stage from Borce. The Tour could then be completed to the Lac de Bious-Artigues and the GR 10 continued to Gourette on the following day. This would however make two very long, hard days. Considering the beauty of the surroundings, it is preferable to linger in this area.

Reverse yesterday's route from the Lac de Bious-Artigues to the Plaine de Bious. Just before a footbridge over a stream the path divides. Take the left-hand branch and cross the bridge. Soon begin a zig-zagged ascent through woodland and continue on a clear path to the Lac de Peyreget. From here there is a choice of two routes. Either make

Lac de Peyreget

a circuit of the southern flanks of the Pic de Peyreget via the Col de l'Iou to the Refuge de Pombie, or a better and shorter way is via the Col de Peyreget. This latter route involves a little easy scrambling over huge boulders and provides a close-up view of the rock faces of the 'Petit Pic'. Climb up from the Lac de Peyreget, first over grass and then scrambling over rocks, following faint paint marks and small cairns to the top of the pass. Here at the Col de Peyreget (7554ft;2300m) look down to the Pombie hut below. Isard are often sighted in this area. Descend passing a small tarn to the Lake and Refuge of Pombie (CAF).

From the refuge take a clear path heading generally in a north-easterly direction, skirting the crags of the 'Grand Pic', and climb to the Col de Suzon (6985ft;2127m). From here an ascent of the Pic de Midi d'Ossau (or Jean-Pierre as it is affectionately known) by the 'normal' route can be made. However this is for experienced scramblers or rock climbers only and should not be attempted by anyone inexperienced in rock work. There are often several parties on this route and consequently there is danger from rockfall.

To continue on the standard Tour descend the upper levels of the Magnabaigt valley on a clear path, crossing a stream near a cascade and eventually reach the Col Long de Magnabaigt. From here go down

The view from below the Col de Suzon

through pleasant woodland to the car park to return to the starting point at the Chalet du Club Pyrénéa Sports.

SECTION 2: DAY 5

LAC DE BIOUS-ARTIGUES to GOURETTE

DISTANCE:	$16^{1/2}$ miles	(26.6km)
ASCENT:	4864ft	(1481m)
DESCENT:	5097ft	(1552m)

	Timings					
	Sect.	Accum.	Shop	Bar/ Café	Restau- rant	Accomm- odation
LAC DE BIOUS-ARTIGUES			(+)	-	-	R. (CP)
GABAS	.50	.50	-	+	+	G. H+
CORNICHE DES ALHAS	1.15	2.05	-	-	-	-
HOURQUETTE D'ARRE	4.30	6.35	-	-	-	-
LAC D'ANGLAS	.50	7.25	-	-	-	-
GOURETTE	1.30	8.55	++	++	++	R+. H+. (CP)

There are two refuges in Gourette, the Chalet-Skier du Club Pyrénéa Sports and the Chalet du Club Alpin Français. There are numerous hotels in this fashionable winter and summer resort. Gabas has a National Park Office and a Tourist Information Office.

At Laruns, 7½ miles (12km) from Gabas down the Vallée d'Ossau, it is possible to catch a bus to Busy, south of Pau where there is a main-line railway station.

This is a hard day, particularly during the last stages of the climb to the Hourquette d'Arre, but the scenery is first rate. Late snow can be a considerable problem on this section. There is little opportunity for obtaining water on much of this route.

Descend the D 231 road, pass the campsite and continue for about 2½ miles (4km) to the crossroads at the N 134. Turn left here to enter the small village of Gabas, but for the GR 10 turn right and walk eastwards up the road for 15 minutes to the hydro-electric power station. From here take the waymarked path on the left into the woods. This path heads west for a while before turning north. Do not take any side turnings but continue until the path joins a forestry track. After about 450 yards take a path off to the right to walk along the impressive Corniche des Alhas. If this path is missed then the forestry track can be followed downhill to a bridge over the river and climbed steeply to rejoin the standard route after the Corniche des Alhas. Note: the Corniche des Alhas path is signposted as "Vertigineux" and should not be attempted in poor conditions or by those unsure of their abilities - in such cases use the lower route instead.

Climb above the tree line and continue on in an easterly direction on a well defined, almost level footpath for several miles. There are several copper mines in this area; the footpath was built in order to transport copper ore. There are superb views here, the distinctive shape of the Pic du Midi d'Ossau dominating the scene. Unfortunately the path begins to climb once more to cross a river three times in all. Leave the river and pass the low walls of a small ruined building. The waymarks are difficult to find in this area but the destination should never be in doubt. Head ever upwards towards the approaching col, finally climbing the steep scree slopes to the top of the Hourquette d' Arre. Readers are advised to avoid ascending the final stage of the snow field immediately below (the west side of) the Hourquette d'Arre. It becomes very steep and potentially dangerous. The very sharp and loose scree is a safer route. This col at 8095ft (2465m) is the highest

'Chemin Horizontal' on the way to the Hourquette d'Arre

point on the GR 10 thus far. The col is so steep that the panorama to the east is out of view until the very top is attained.

Descend heading to the north-east on a good but steep path to the ruined building near to the Lac d'Anglas. Continue the descent now heading in a northerly direction down the left-hand side of the valley until the multi-storied buildings of the ski-resort of Gourette come into view. Drop down to the streets of this town where several shops, restaurants and cafés will be found. The campsite is over half a mile away and 700ft (213m) below Gourette on the Plateau de Ley (follow the N 618 out of the town).

INTRODUCTION

The Hautes Pyrénées contains some of the most spectacular and best known mountain scenery in the Pyrenees. Much of the area belonged to the old medieval division of Bigorre and several of the place names in the region still bear this title. From Gourette the GR 10 crosses to Arrens and then takes a route to the north of the Balaïtous massif to cross the Col d'Ilhéou on the boundary of the Pyrenean National Park before descending to Cauterets. There are then two alternative routes between Cauterets and the other major town in the area, Luz-Saint-Sauveur. The standard route is a short day's walk over the Col de Riou, but the variation via the Hourquette d'Ossoue and Gavarnie will take three days to accomplish. However the latter route is by far the more scenic, providing views of the giant Vignemale (10,831ft;3298m) and its glacier as well as giving an opportunity to see the deservedly famous Cirque de Gavarnie. If time is available it would thus be foolish to take the shorter route and miss the splendours of the high mountains in the National Park. However in bad weather it would be unwise to follow the southern variation and it should be noted that snow lies on the high passes for much of the year.

The high-level variation of the GR 10 leaves the fashionable spa resort of Cauterets and passes many waterfalls on its way to the Pont d'Espagne and the Lac de Gaube from where Vignemale, the highest of all the peaks on the frontier, will be seen. The Hourquette d'Ossoue, at 8979ft (2734m) the highest col on the GR 10, must be crossed before Gavarnie is reached. The latter is the traditional headquarters of Pyrénéisme, mountaineering in the Pyrenees, and tourists have been going there for centuries to visit the famous Cirque de Gavarnie. It really is a most impressive site, the giant wall of the Cirque rising some 1500m above the valley floor in three distinct layers of limestone. The enormous waterfall which cascades down the face of the Cirque is the origin of the Gave de Pau which leads back to Luz-Saint-Sauveur. The large cleft in the Cirque is the Breche de Roland situated on the border and this allows access into the Ordesa National Park in Spain and to Monte Perdido, the lost mountain. There are two other cirques in the neighbourhood which are worth a visit, the Cirque d'Estaubé and the Cirque de Troumouse. The latter is accessible from Gèdre and is very fine, but suffers from being overshadowed by its more illustrious neighbour.

Luz-Saint-Sauveur is really two towns. Luz is a small pleasant resort and Saint-Sauveur is a separate spa a couple of kilometres away. The latter was visited by Napoléon in 1859 and this led to the construction of the gigantic Pont Napoléon over which the GR 10 passes on its way to Barèges, a small ski resort higher up the valley of the River Bastan. The route then heads towards the Col du Tourmalet which has the distinction of being the highest road pass in the Pyrenees. From the Col it is possible to walk or take a cable car to the top of the Pic du Midi de Bigorre, a mountain disfigured by the large observatory on its summit. The GR 10, however, traverses the Col de Madamète to enter what could be described as the Pyrenean Lake District, a region of high granite peaks including the Pic de Néouvielle (10,151ft;3091m) and Pic Long (10,483ft;3192m). The latter is the highest summit in the Pyrenees on the French side of the border. Here is a rather austere, rocky landscape dotted with numerous deep mountain lakes. The area is a nature reserve. After passing Lac d'Aubert and Lac d'Aumar the route descends to the Lac de l'Oule to leave the National Park for the last time and continue eastwards to descend to the Aure valley.

To the north of the mountains is the best known town in the Pyrenees, Lourdes. This is probably the greatest pilgrimage centre of Roman Catholicism and receives some four million visitors each year. It can be easily reached by bus from Luz-Saint-Sauveur. The chief town of the region is Tarbes which has little to offer the visitor other than a main-line railway station.

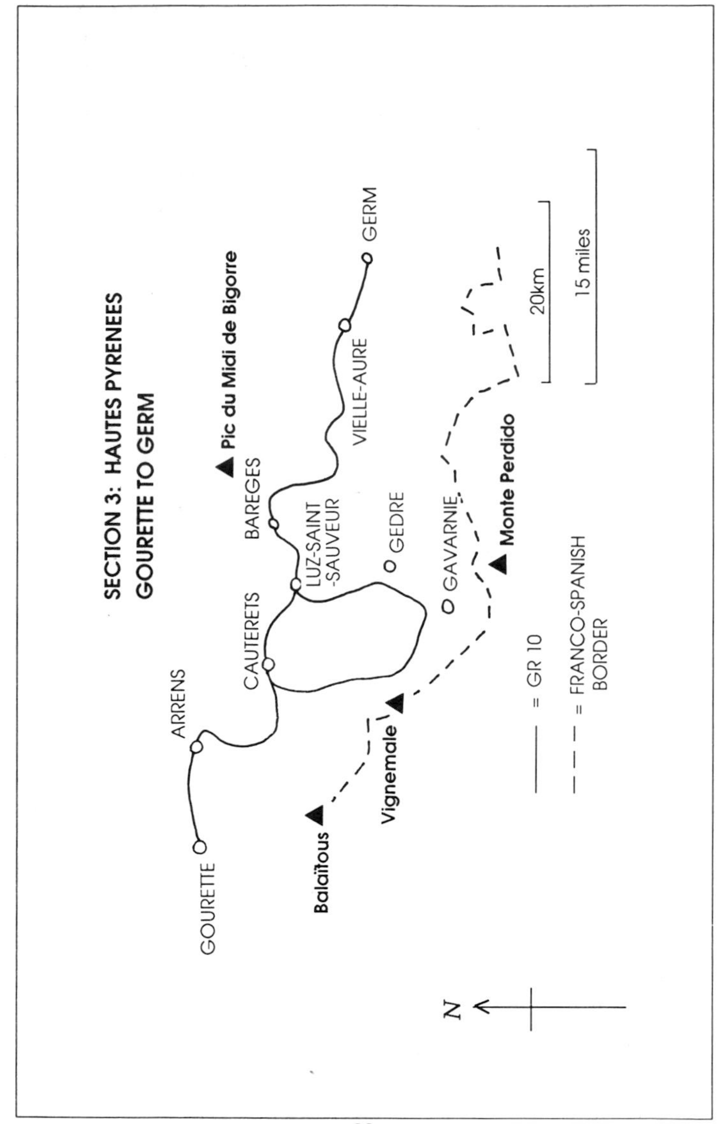
SECTION 3: HAUTES PYRENEES
GOURETTE TO GERM
Pic du Midi de Bigorre
GERM
VIELLE-AURE
BAREGES
LUZ-SAINT
-SAUVEUR
GEDRE
GAVARNIE
Monte Perdido
CAUTERETS
ARRENS
GOURETTE
Balaïtous
Vignemale
20km
15 miles
= GR 10
= FRANCO-SPANISH
BORDER
N

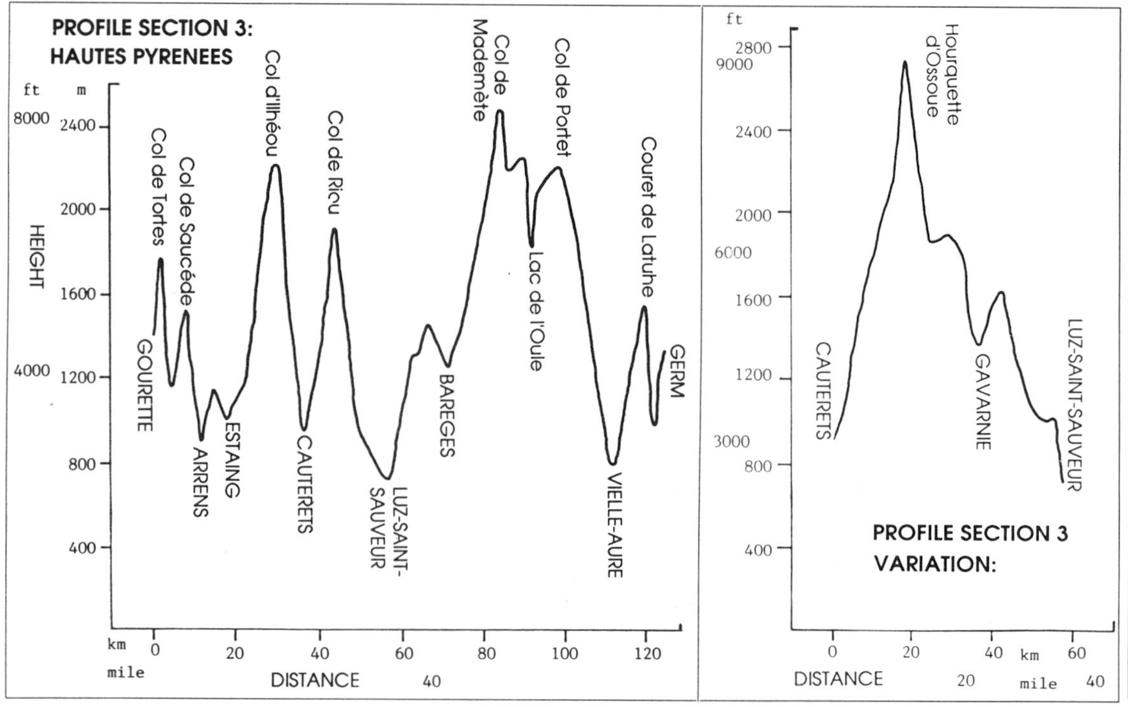
PROFILE SECTION 3:
HAUTES PYRENEES
HEIGHT
ft
m
8000
2400
2000
1600
4000
1200
800
400
GOURETTE
Col de Tortes
Col de Saucéde
ARRENS
ESTAING
Col d'Ilhéou
CAUTERETS
Col de Ricu
LUZ-SAINT-
SAUVEUR
BAREGES
Col de
Mademète
Lac de l'Oule
Col de Portet
VIELLE-AURE
Couret de Latuhe
GERM
km
0
20
40
60
80
100
120
mile
DISTANCE
40
ft
2800
9000
2400
2000
6000
1600
1200
3000
800
400
Hourquette
d'Ossoue
CAUTERETS
GAVARNIE
LUZ-SAINT-SAUVEUR
PROFILE SECTION 3
VARIATION:
0
20
40
km
60
DISTANCE
20
mile
40

SECTION 3: DAY 1

GOURETTE to ARRENS

DISTANCE:	$7^{1/2}$ miles	(12.1km)
ASCENT:	1931ft	(588m)
DESCENT:	3468ft	(1056m)

	Timings					
	Sect.	Accum.	Shop	Bar/ Café	Restau- rant	Accomm- odation
GOURETTE			++	++	++	R+. H+. (CP)
COL DE TORTES	1.20	1.20	-	-	-	-
R.N. 618	1.00	2.20	-	-	-	-
COL DE SAUCEDE	1.20	3.40	-	-	-	-
ARRENS	2.00	5.40	++	++	++	G+. Y. H+. CP+

A short but neither an over strenuous nor particularly inspiring day. There is a short section along a rather busy main road. Time may permit a part of tomorrow's route to be completed (eg to the gîte d'étape at Viellette), thus cutting tomorrow's rather hard day to a more manageable length.

Leave Gourette on the N 618 road in the direction signposted Col d'Aubisque. About 300 yards past the last house take a footpath off to the right. Follow the red/white markings as the path climbs fairly steeply at first, through trees and then on open hillside to reach the Col de Tortes (5908ft;1799m). Descend on the marked path, ensuring that the right-hand, waymarked path is followed at about the half-way mark on the descent. This path descends to the road (RN 618, one of the most spectacular mountain roads in France).

Turn right and follow the road for about $1^{1/2}$ miles (2.4km). This is a rather busy road during the holiday season. At the first road tunnel take the path to the left, i.e. do not walk through the tunnel. Note that although the path to the left of the first tunnel is not inherently difficult, it is nevertheless quite exposed. For this reason several walkers opt to take the tunnel route notwithstanding its competing risk. Continue along the road to pass through a second short tunnel and then, about 700 yards after a small bridge, at the boundary of the départements of Pyrénées-Atlantiques and Hautes-Pyrénées where the road turns to climb northwards, take a waymarked path leading east. Climb to the Col de Saucède (5008ft;1525m). From here continue eastwards (the grassy track heading north-eastwards leads to the Col de Soulor where there are cafés and restaurants). The path eventually becomes a track which is well signposted down to the Pont de la Badéte. Continue along the road into Arrens where several shops, hotels, gîte d'étapes, campsites, cafés, restaurants and a Tourist Information Office will be found. It may be possible to catch a bus from here to Lourdes. (The gîte d'étape called "Camelat" in Arrens provides outstanding meals at modest cost.)

SECTION 3: DAY 2
ARRENS to CAUTERETS

DISTANCE:	15 miles	(24.2km)
ASCENT:	5005ft	(1524m)
DESCENT:	4890ft	(1489m)

	Timings Sect.	Accum.	Shop	Bar/ Café	Restau- rant	Accomm- odation
ARRENS			++	++	++	G+. Y. H+. CP+
COL DES BORDERES	.55	.55	-	-	-	-
VIELLETTE	1.15	2.10	-	-	-	G
LAC D'ESTAING	.40	2.50	-	-	+	H. CP
COL D'ILHEOU	3.40	6.30	-	-	-	-
LAC D'ILHEOU	.50	7.20	-	-	-	R
CAUTERETS	2.30	9.50	++	++	++	G. H+. CP+

An enjoyable section, particularly the stage over the high mountain pass of the Col d'Ilhéou. This rather long day could be easily shortened by staying a night at the Raymond Ritter Refuge at the Lac d'Ilhéou.

From Arrens retrace the route back to the Pont de la Badéte. Follow the red/white waymarks over an old bridge and up a series of zig-zags on tracks and narrow paths, rejoining the road at intervals. When the climb is over the route joins the road at the Col des Bordères (3777ft;1150m). The GR 10 leaves and joins the road several times from here on as it makes its way to the small village of Estaing (no shop). Follow the route as it gradually climbs the Estaing valley to reach

Viellette where there is a gîte d'étape. There are also two campsites on the road between Estaing and Viellette. Continue on up the valley to reach the Lac d'Estaing. No wild camping is allowed at this picturesque tourist spot, but there is a campsite at the far end of the lake (no provisions available but a restaurant / café / bar serves meals and snacks. Also a baker's van arives on the site at c. 8.30 each morning). Also, the hotel just before the lake provides good, albeit rather expensive meals.

Take the path leading up from the lakeside signposted 'Cauterets via Col d'Ilhéou (6hrs 30mins)'. Climb steeply up through the forest to emerge on open mountainside with a river below on the right. After crossing the river ascend steeply by a series of well marked zig-zags to the Col d'Ilhéou at 7363ft (2242m). Leave this wide, open, relatively flat col in an easterly direction to pass two cabanes (one of metal and the other of stone). Turn towards the south and descend to the Lac d'Ilhéou and the Refuge Raymond Ritter (6486ft;1975m). This refuge is on the boundary of the National Park and provides evening meals and drinks and snacks during the day. Note that there is an alternative path that does not pass the refuge.

From the refuge head in a northerly direction to pass above the tiny Lac Noir. Follow the Gave d'Ilhéou down a route well waymarked with red/white flashes, roughly following the boundary of the National Park. It is easy to lose the official route and walk down a clear, wide track. Do not worry overduly if this happens as both the track and the official GR 10 route will eventually lead to an area of woodland. Descend steeply through this to emerge at a road in Cauterets (2998ft;913m). Turn right here for the town centre where there are numerous shops, hotels, restaurants and a gîte d'étape. There are also several campsites and a Tourist Information Office in this spa town. A bus may be taken from here to Pierrefitte-Nestalas and on to Lourdes where there is a main-line railway station. There is a Mountain Guides office in Cauterets where staff can advise on the snow conditions on the Hourquette d'Ossoue and provide a weather forecast.

SECTION 3: DAY 3

CAUTERETS to LUZ-SAINT-SAUVEUR

DISTANCE:	$11^{1}/_{2}$ miles	(18.5km)
ASCENT:	3402ft	(1036m)
DESCENT:	4036ft	(1229m)

	Timings Sect.	Accum.	Shop	Bar/ Café	Restau-rant	Accomm-odation
CAUTERETS			++	++	++	G. H+. CP+
CHAL. DE LA REINE HORTENSE	.45	.45	-	-	+	-
COL DE RIOU	2.10	2.55	-	-	-	-
GRUST	2.30	5.25	-	-	-	A
LUZ-SAINT-SAUVEUR	1.15	6.40	++	++	++	G. H+. CP

This is the standard route from Cauterets to Luz-Saint-Sauveur via the Col de Riou. For the much longer, but more spectacular route via Gavarnie see the Variation given at the end of Section 3 (page 93).

Near the centre of Cauterets find the Thermes de César. Take a path up to the left of these baths and zig-zag up to a metalled road. This becomes a track and leads up to the Chalet de la Reine Hortense, a restaurant overlooking Cauterets, offering a fine view of the valley which leads eventually to Lourdes. Continue upwards through the forest following the signs to the Col de Riou. After about 50 minutes emerge from the trees to reach a shepherd's cottage (Clairière) at about 4844ft (1475m) where water may be available. Continue up the mountainside on a well waymarked path, ascending seemingly endless zig-zags to emerge at the Col de Riou (6401ft;1949m) where there is a large derelict house.

Walk over the col following the waymarks first to the north-east and then to the south-west to cross a skiing area, then descend to a roadhead. Follow the road on its descent to the valley, but take several waymarked short-cuts to avoid many of the hairpin bends in the road. Eventually leave the road for a series of narrow paths which lead to Grust, a small village situated above the valley. There is a small auberge in the village which may provide food and lodging for the night. Continue to pass through the village of Sazos (small grocer's shop) and make the long descent, mainly on the D 12 road, to the valley below.

On reaching a road junction continue ahead, crossing a road bridge to enter the town of Luz-Saint-Sauveur (2365ft;720m). For the nearest campsite turn left at the road junction and walk for about half a mile where the campsite will be found on the right-hand side of the road. Luz-Saint-Sauveur is a fairly large town offering numerous facilities for shopping and sleeping, including a gîte d'étape. There is a Tourist Information Office and a bus service down the valley to Lourdes (for the SNCF main-line station) and up the valley to Barèges (tomorrow's destination).

SECTION 3: DAY 4

LUZ-SAINT-SAUVEUR to BAREGES

DISTANCE:	10.2 miles	(16.4km)
ASCENT:	2519ft	(767m)
DESCENT:	811ft	(247m)

	Timings					
	Sect.	Accum.	Shop	Bar/ Café	Restau- rant	Accomm- odation
LUZ-SAINT-SAUVEUR			++	++	++	G. H+. CP+
PONT NAPOLEON	.40	.40	+	-	-	-
RIVER CROSSING	3.20	4.00	-	-	-	(G)
BAREGES	1.15	5.15	++	++	++	G. H+. CP

Another short stage, being little more than a half-day's walk. The section climbs above the valley floor, but generally follows the direction of the valley to descend eventually to the winter sports town of Barèges. This stage could easily be omitted by taking the daily bus up the valley.

Walk along the road in a south-easterly direction, first on the D 912 and then on the N 21 through the spa town of Saint-Sauveur (really a suburb of Luz), passing the thermal baths to reach the impressive Pont Napoléon. Cross the bridge then the main road and take a small path leaving the road almost opposite the junction. This climbs and leads up to a church to skirt above Luz and pass through the hamlet of Villenave. The narrow path then climbs steeply through woodland and hedgerow to emerge onto open hillside giving good views of Luz in the valley below. Next the route skirts the hillside above the valley on a more or less level path, before climbing again to head in a south-easterly direction with the river below and to the left. A sign will be reached indicating the way to the gîte d'étape du Bôlou, about 15 minutes walk from the GR 10. Take care in this area as there are many footpaths and tracks serving a number of bergeries.

Cross the river by a ford at the spot marked as Bôlou on the 1:50,000 IGN map (4795ft;1460m) and turn to proceed in a north-north-easterly direction following a good path. After some time come to a path junction where Barèges is signposted down to the left. Follow this, soon entering trees. The path becomes a smooth forest track leading down to the high street of Barèges. Here many facilities may be found including a gîte d'étape (Hospitalet de Barèges), shops, restaurants and a Tourist Information Office. Make the most of these as no others will be seen for two days! The campsite is below the village on the main road (N 618), about a 10-minute-walk from the centre.

3000m peaks from the Col de Madamète

SECTION 3: DAY 5

BAREGES to LAC DE L'OULE

DISTANCE:	12.7 miles	(20.4km)
ASCENT:	4391ft	(1337m)
DESCENT:	2483ft	(756m)

	Timings Sect.	Accum.	Shop	Bar/ Café	Restau- rant	Accomm- odation
BAREGES			++	++	++	G. H+. CP
PONT DE LA GAUBIE	1.10	1.10	-	+	+	-
CABANE D'AYGUES-CLUSES	2.30	3.40	-	-	-	C
COL DE MADAMETE	1.0	4.40	-	-	-	-
ROUTE DES LACS	1.10	5.50	-	-	-	(H)
COL D'ESTOUDOU	1.15	7.05	-	-	-	-
LAC DE L'OULE	.55	8.00	-	-	-	-
CHALET-HOTEL DE L'OULE	.15	8.15	-	-	-	R. H.

The next two days provide some of the finest walking on the central section of the GR 10. The landscape is wild, rugged and largely uninhabited; the scenery in this 'land of the lakes' is of a very high order. If it was not for the road (Route des Lacs) much used by tourists, this would indeed be a wilderness area. The walking is quite strenuous and for the first time on the GR 10 there is somewhat of an accommodation problem. The stage ends at the Chalet-Hôtel de l'Oule which is at the southern end of the Lac de l'Oule and a short detour from the GR 10. The only alternative to this hotel / refuge would be to continue on tomorrow's itinerary and make another diversion, to the Refuge de Bastanet, although this would make for quite a long day. Backpackers carrying their own tent will have no real problems as water is fairly abundant. Ensure that sufficient food is carried as the next grocer's shop is in Vielle-Aure, two days' walk from Barèges.

Leave Barèges heading east-north-east on the N 918 in the direction of the Col du Tourmalet (alternatively follow a marked path which runs close to the road and joins it after about half a mile). Continue on the road for just under 2 miles. At the junction to Super-Barèges take the left fork. After crossing a small bridge bear right and follow the river, heading in a southerly direction towards the Café-Restaurant

Lac d'Aubert and Lac d'Aumar

of La Gaubie situated behind a clump of fir trees (a good place for a second breakfast!).

After the café continue ascending in a southerly direction for about half an hour until, near to a small bridge, a signpost is reached indicating a parting of the ways. This spot is marked as 'Pountou' on the 1:50,000 IGN map. Take the path signposted to the Col de Madamète (3hrs 30mins). Follow an obvious path climbing steadily up the Vallée d'Aygues-Cluses, until the Cabane d'Aygues-Cluses (7061ft;2150m) comes into view. This is a small unguarded shelter by the Lac de Coueyla-Gran, capable of accommodating up to six people. (It has been reported that the cabane is now used to shelter animals and is consequently quite unsuitable for overnight accommodation.)

From here head south, climbing more steeply to pass a series of three small lakes (Lacs de Madamète). The route turns slightly to head south-west. Clamber over several boulders and rocks to reach the Col de Madamète at 8240ft (2509m). Here between the Pic de Madamète and the Pic d'Estibère, a marvelous vista opens out. To the north is the Pic du Midi de Bigorre (9432ft;2872m) with its conspicuous TV relay station. To the south-west lies a range of 3000m+ peaks towering above numerous lakes and tarns. The most prominent summits are the Pic de Néouvielle (10,151ft;3091m) and Pic Long (10,483ft;3192m). The mighty Monte Perdido (11,018ft;3355m) lies beyond, across the border inside Spain.

Descend from the col to enter the National Nature Reserve of Néouvielle. In this region there are many lakes, several of then artificial with impressive dams. Descend over large rocks and boulders to pass to the left of a small tarn (Gourg de Rabas) and continue until the road is reached, where you turn left. This is the Route des Lacs which in this region passes between two large picturesque lakes (Lac d'Aubert and Lac d'Aumar). The area is popular with holidaymakers and during the main season picnic parties will be passed on the shores of the lake. If shelter is essential then follow the road downhill for about 45 minutes to an hotel (plus dormitory accommodation) close to the Lac d'Orédon. However the GR 10 does not go here, but soon leaves the road to take a waymarked path off to the left. Follow an undulating route through woodland with fine views below and to the right of several dammed lakes. After the Col d'Estoudou (7422ft;2260m) descend steeply to the east through more woodland to emerge on a track in front of the Lac de l'Oule. For the Chalet-Hôtel de l'Oule, turn right on this track and follow the lakeside, heading south-east for about 15 minutes. The GR 10, however, turns to the left (north) on meeting the Lac de l'Oule.

SECTION 3: DAY 6

LAC DE L'OULE to VIELLE-AURE

DISTANCE:	12.2 miles	(19.6km)
ASCENT:	1294ft	(394m)
DESCENT:	4647ft	(1415m)

	Timings Sect.	Timings Accum.	Shop	Bar/ Café	Restau- rant	Accomm- odation
CHALET-HOTEL DE L'OULE			-	-	-	R.H.
JUNCTION WITH THE GR 10 C	1.30	1.30	-	-	-	(R)
COL DE PORTET	1.20	2.50	-	-	-	C
VIELLE-AURE	3.30	6.20	++	++	++	G. Y. H+

Return along the lakeside to rejoin the GR 10. Continue along the track with the lake on the right until the northern end of the lake is reached. Here follow red / white waymarks to climb steeply above the lake to reach a signpost at 6930ft (2110m) indicating a parting of the ways. The path to the left follows the GR 10 C (a variant of the main route which heads northwards for about 8½ miles (13.7km) through an area of lakes and tarns to descend eventually to the Vallée de Gripp). About 30 minutes along the GR 10 C leads to the Refuge de Bastanet (7356ft;2240m) which has a warden during the summer months.

After the junction with the GR 10 C, the main GR 10 continues for a while on a more or less level footpath along the hillside, first going in a southerly direction above the Lac de l'Oule and then in a north-easterly direction until a stream is crossed. Here the route turns south again before finally climbing again in an easterly direction to reach the Col de Portet (7274ft;2215m). If the exact route is mislaid in this area, the walker should eventually reach a wide ski-track. Turning left uphill on this will lead to the Col de Portet. As well as a ski-lift, this col also boasts a small cabane with a sleeping area and a fireplace with chimney (will accommodate up to four people).

From the Col de Portet descend to a river then continue in an easterly direction, slowly descending for many miles. The path is fairly well defined. Eventually descend more steeply with a fence on the right. Leaving this enter woodland and descend very steeply for some way until emerging above the town of Vielle-Aure. Continue the steep descent crossing the road twice before entering the village. Follow the signs to the gîte d'étape.

From Vielle-Aure there is a daily bus service down the Vallée d'Aure to Arreau where other buses can be taken to Tarbes or Lannemezan (for SNCF main-line station). The busy little town of St. Lary lies only a mile to the south of Vielle-Aure. All facilities will be found in St. Lary which can be recommened for a rest day, as there is plenty to do in the town, including taking a spectacular telepherique up the mountainside.

SECTION 3: DAY 7

VIELLE-AURE to GERM

DISTANCE:	8.1 miles	(13km)
ASCENT:	3793ft	(1155m)
DESCENT:	2023ft	(616m)

	Timings Sect.	Accum.	Shop	Bar/ Café	Restau-rant	Accomm-odation
VIELLE-AURE			++	++	++	G. Y. H+.
BOURISP	.15	.15	-	-	-	-
AZET	1.05	1.20	-	-	+	G. H.
COURET DE LATUHE	1.20	2.40	-	-	-	-
LOUDENVIELLE	1.25	4.05	++	++	++	H+ (G) (CP)
GERM	1.00	5.05	-	-	-	G/Y

A short stage, really little more than a half-day's walk, but through some charming villages and with a pleasant gîte d'étape for an overnight stay. Loudenvielle is a good place to stock up on foodstuffs for the next section of the journey.

Walk through the old streets of Vielle-Aure to cross the bridge and continue along the D 116 to the main road (the N 929). Cross this highway and enter Bourisp, a village with a fine medieval church. Before reaching the church the GR 10 waymarks lead off to the right and the path climbs steeply above the village, heading in a south-easterly direction to emerge on the road at another village, Estensan. After a few hundred yards leave the road by taking a waymarked path on the right and continue to climb until the village of Azet is reached, an historic settlement with a gîte d'étape and an hotel-restaurant (the Auberge du Col).

Pass the church in Azet and then follow the red/white markings to ascend on a good track. This eventually becomes a path as it climbs the hillside heading to the south-east. You will find it unclear in a few places, but if unsure just maintain direction until eventually the Couret de Latuhe is reached at a height of 5209ft (1586m). Here take great care not to follow the variant path heading north-east which is waymarked with red/white flashes and heads to Adervielle. (This diversion is useful, however, if seeking accommodation at the Gîte d'Adervielle des Amis de la Nature. There is also a campsite at Adervielle.) For the GR 10 descend from the Couret de Latuhe mainly in an easterly direction to Loudenvielle (3186ft;970m) in the valley below. The Louron valley has several villages scattered along its length and Loudenvielle is one of the largest. Here there are several cafés, restaurants and hotels. There are several shops and a most useful supermarket. It should be possible to take a bus from here down the valley to Arreau and on to Lannemezan where there is a railway station.

Walk through the town and just before the church take the waymarked path to the left. This climbs steeply through woodland to emerge in the village of Germ (4397ft;1339m). Here there is an interesting Pyrenean church and a gîte d'étape (complete with swimming pool!). The latter provides meals and also doubles as a youth hostel, although it is not necessary to hold a YHA card in order to stay the night. Mention should also be made of a variant route from Loudenvielle (marked on the 1:50,000 IGN map) which avoids Germ to re-join the main GR 10 just before the Cabane d'Ourtiga prior to the climb to the Pas de Couret.

SECTION 3: VARIATION DAY 1

CAUTERETS to REFUGE BAYSSELLANCE

DISTANCE:	11.2 miles	(18km)
ASCENT:	5980ft	(1821m)
DESCENT:	273ft	(83m)

	Timings					
	Sect.	Accum.	Shop	Bar/ Café	Restau- rant	Accomm- odation
CAUTERETS			++	++	++	G. H+. CP+
PONT D'ESPAGNE	1.50	1.50	-	-	+	H
LAC DE GAUBE	.45	2.35	-	-	-	-
REFUGES DES OULETTES DE GAUBE	1.45	4.20	-	-	-	R
HOURQUETTE D'OSSOUE	2.15	6.35	-	-	-	-
REFUGE BAYSSELLANCE	.10	6.45	-	-	-	R

This stage is uphill nearly all the way, but the effort is compensated with some of the finest mountain scenery in the Pyrenees. There are grand views of Vignemale (10,831ft;3298m) and an opportunity to climb the Petit Vignemale from the Hourquette d'Ossoue. The latter, at 8979ft (2734m), has the distinction of being the highest point reached on the GR 10 (with the exception of the Pic du Canigou which is not strictly on the official route of the GR 10). Note that on the highest sections of today's route some small snowfields may be encountered.

Leave Cauterets heading south, climbing to enter the forest of Péguère. Continue to climb through the wood to reach a road and the Thermes de la Raillère. Here there is a restaurant. There are fine views of the Lutour and Jéret waterfalls. These waters are thermal and sulphurous. Turn towards the south-west to climb up the Val de Jéret and enter the National Park. The footpath continues through woodland and alongside thundering cascades to the Pont d'Espagne (4913ft;1496m) where there is a hotel-restaurant. There is also a chalet-refuge some 15 minutes' walk from here. This whole area is very popular with tourists and hill walkers and is likely to be busy during the summer months.

Cross the bridge and soon take a footpath climbing steeply to the south. Ascend on a good path through trees to arrive at the Lac de Gaube (5665ft;1725m). Continue to the upper station of the cable car and follow the west bank of the lake. After the lake continue in a southerly direction to climb along the left bank of the stream. Pass a bridge (do not cross) and a little further on cross the river by a second bridge. From here continue on the right bank of the river to pass the Cabane de Pinet. The angle eventually eases somewhat and the path then re-crosses the stream by a footbridge. Continue now on the left bank of the stream up this glaciated valley until the Refuge des Oulettes de Gaube is reached at 7064ft (2151m). This large CAF refuge is open all the year and meals may be purchased from the resident warden during the summer months. The view from here of the north face of Vignemale is most impressive.

The next section should not be attempted in adverse weather or if there is considerable snow still lying on the approaches to the pass. If in doubt ask the guardian of the refuge for advice. From the refuge take the footpath which climbs above the plateau by numerous zig-zags. At 7997ft (2435m) the path divides. The path to the left leads to the Col d'Arraillé, but the GR 10 takes the right-hand path climbing towards the south-east and then the south. Negotiate several zig-zags to reach at long last the Hourquette d'Ossoue (8979ft;2734m). This high-level col separating the valleys of the Ossoue and Gaube presents first-rate views of the Cirque de Gavarnie. From this col it is possible to make an ascent of the Petit Vignemale and so cross the magical 3000m mark. The Petit Vignemale stands at 9958ft (3032m) and its ascent requires about 45 minutes' effort from the Hourquette d'Ossoue.

A short, steep descent from the Hourquette leads to the Refuge Bayssellance. This CAF hut at 8706ft (2651m) is the highest refuge in the Pyrenees. It has a resident guardian during the main season, but a part of the building remains open all the year. Meals are provided.

SECTION 3: VARIATION DAY 2

REFUGE BAYSSELLANCE to GAVARNIE

DISTANCE:	$11^{1/2}$ miles	(18.5km)
ASCENT:	463ft	(141m)
DESCENT:	4686ft	(1427m)

	Timings Sect.	Accum.	Shop	Bar/ Café	Restau- rant	Accomm- odation
REFUGE BAYSSELLANCE			-	-	-	R
OULETTES D'OSSOUE	2.10	2.10	-	-	-	-
SAUSSE-DESSUS	2.00	4.10	-	-	-	-
PONT DE SAINT-SAVIN	1.50	6.00	-	-	-	(R)
GAVARNIE	.25	6.25	++	++	++	H+

Today is the opposite of yesterdays route in that it is nearly all descent. The day is not overlong and hence there is opportunity to savour the superb surroundings of this deservedly famous area. The day ends at the well known mountain village of Gavarnie where there are several hotels and shops. It is possible to take a bus from here to Lourdes and Tarbes. Alternatively a night could be spent at the mountain refuge Chalet de Holle, without visiting Gavarnie.

The Refuge Bayssellance is the starting point for the ascent of

Vignemale by way of the Glacier d'Ossoue, but leave the climbers to their sport and descend on a good footpath, zig-zagging at times to pass in front of the Grottes de Bellevue. These could provide spartan shelter if required, but the GR 10 continues to descend numerous zig-zags. This requires some care but the way is always obvious and leads eventually to the Oulettes d'Ossoue (6128ft;1866m).

Continue in a south-easterly direction until the Barrage d'Ossoue is reached. Near here is a small cabane which is usually open. It is possible to take a track from here which leads directly to Gavarnie in about 5 miles (8km). This is clearly marked on the IGN 1:50,000 map. The GR 10, however, crosses a footbridge and ascends a little towards the south then continues on a well waymarked path to pass a shepherd's hut. A stream is crossed by means of a footbridge and the route then goes to the north and later to the east to reach the Saussé-Dessus valley. Here there is another cabane.

Cross the stream over a footbridge and traverse a flat grassy area heading towards the north. The route gradually swings towards the east. Several small streams are crossed and the path soon leaves the National Park. The way continues to descend towards the east, partly through woodland and partly over grassy hillsides ripe with azaleas, to reach a road. Turning left on this will lead eventually to Gavarnie. However, for the GR 10 leave this road at the first hairpin bend and descend to the Praire de Holle (4861ft;1480m) where there is a small CAF refuge. Continue the descent to the Pont de Saint-Savin. Cross the bridge over the Gave d'Ossoue, follow the left bank of the river for about 300 yards and ascend to the road. Cross the road and take the footpath to continue the GR 10, but for Gavarnie (4483ft;1365m) turn right at this road and follow it down into the village.

Limestone scenery below Hourquette d'Arre

On the ascent of the Col de Madamète

'Land of the Lakes' from Col de Madamète

SECTION 3: VARIATION DAY 3

GAVARNIE to LUZ-SAINT-SAUVEUR

DISTANCE:	13 miles	(20.9km)
ASCENT:	985ft	(300m)
DESCENT:	3104ft	(945m)

	Timings Sect.	Accum.	Shop	Bar/ Café	Restau- rant	Accomm- odation
GAVARNIE			++	++	++	H+
SAUSSA	2.30	2.30	-	-	-	(H+. CP+)
PRAGNERES	2.00	4.30	-	-	-	-
LUZ-SAINT-SAUVEUR	1.25	5.55	++	++	++	G. H+. CP.

The route now heads north away from the Spanish border to rejoin the standard route at Luz-Saint-Sauveur. The views back to the Cirques of Gavarnie and Troumouse are excellent.

From Gavarnie return on the road to the point where the GR 10 was left yesterday (or if staying at the Refuge de Holle continue on the GR 10 to descend to the Pont de Saint-Savin and cross the river to reach the road). Climb at first towards the east to pass under the HT electricity lines. The line of pylons is then followed for some way. After the Granges de Saugue there is a discrepancy between the line of the GR 10 marked on the 1:50,000 and 1:25,000 IGN maps, and the red / white GR waymarkings. At the point where the route of the GR 10 is shown to take a sharp turn to the east (north of the Hount d'Ourious) to pass under the HT cables before turning to the north again, there are quite fresh (1988) red / white flashes heading north to meet a road near Hount Hérede. Thus the waymarked route does not pass under the HT cables. The new waymarked route then heads off towards Suberpeyre. The line of the GR 10 as marked on the maps should be followed and not the new GR markings. If difficulties are experienced in this region it is advisable to take the minor road down to Sàussa and continue the route from there. Note that there is a thatched, attractive gîte d'étape at Saugué, about 1½ hours after the Pont de Saint Savin (drinks and snacks available here during the day).

Leave the hamlet of Sàussa and re-join the road which leads down

Vallée de Gavarnie

to the busy little town of Gèdre where there are several hotels and campsites. However the GR 10 leaves this road before reaching Gèdre. Take another road leading to the hamlet of Ayrues and on to Pujo. Maintain direction, cross the Pont de Burret and enter yet another hamlet, Trimbareilles (3284ft;1000m). Leave the road on a footpath which leads down through woodland to join the valley road at the Pragnères electricity power station. This is a rather ugly intrusion on the landscape. If staying in Gèdre it is more convenient to reach Pragnères by following a valley path close to the Gave de Pau.

Take the N21 road going north. After a while leave this on the left to climb above the road. Continue to the hamlet of Sia and from here make for the Croix de Sia, a wooden cross erected at the highest point on the footpath (3366ft;1025m). Descend through woodland and continue in a northerly direction. Ignore a path to the left which heads towards Sassis, but instead descend to the road and the thermal baths at Saint-Sauveur. Here turn right to continue the GR 10 to the Pont Napoléon, or turn left to descend to the centre of the town of Luz-Saint-Sauveur whose numerous facilities include two banks.

INTRODUCTION

The département of the Haute Garonne covers a large area stretching north from the Spanish border to include the city of Toulouse, but it is curiously wedge-shaped resulting in only a relatively small area of the Pyrenees being included. The GR 10 passes to the north of the Spanish Posets and Maladetta ranges as it threads its way through the old county of Comminges in what is now the Haute Garonne. The scenery is of the highest order, particularly over to the soaring peaks on the frontier where the highest mountain in the Pyrenees, the Pic d'Aneto, is to be found.

The département takes its name from the River Garonne, one of the great rivers of France. The river rises in the central Pyrenees and soon widens as it flows first to the north-east to Toulouse and then west to the Atlantic at Bordeaux. The upper valley of the River Garonne in the Pyrenees is referred to as the Val d'Aran.

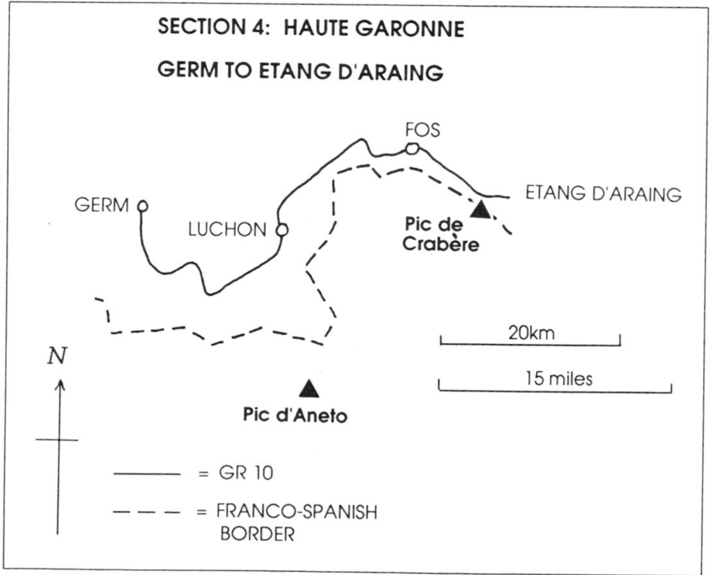

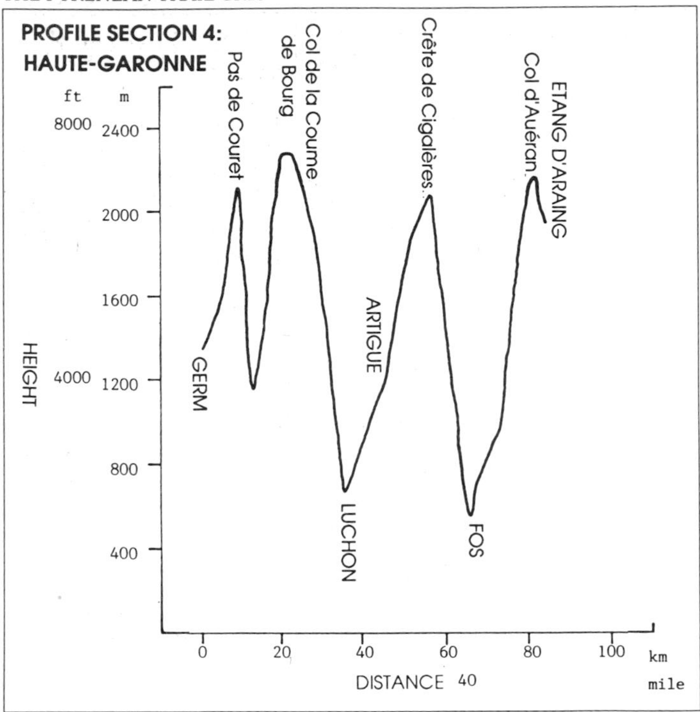

The GR 10 skirts the oddly named Lac d'Oô on its way to Espingo. This is a most attractive mountain lake situated in wild surroundings below the towering summits of the Pic des Crabioules and Pic Perdiguère, two 3000m+ peaks on the Franco-Spanish border. The lake is fed by a most impressive 900ft (274m) waterfall.

The GR 10 passes the ski-complex of Superbagnères with its large Grand Hotel built in the 1920's, before descending to Bagnères-de-Luchon. The town of Luchon dominates this stage of the walk. It became a famous place in the 18th century for 'taking the waters' and the spa town today retains a chic atmosphere. It is quite the smartest town on the GR 10 if not in the whole Pyrenees. There are public parks to sit in, an attractive central boulevard to wander up and down and a busy Saturday market to enjoy. It is a good place to terminate or start a section of the GR 10 as it has excellent rail connections with

Paris, or alternatively it provides a relaxing atmosphere for a rest day or two. The annual Fête des Fleurs is held in August and attracts many tourists to the town.

The country to the north of Luchon is also worth a visit, particularly the hills of the Comminges and the Church of Saint-Bertrand-de-Comminges, one of the most famous religious buildings in the Pyrenees. Finally, if wishing to terminate the GR 10 in Luchon but wanting to visit Spain before returning home, then the historic path past the ruins of the Hospice de France into the Maladetta provides a classic route.

SECTION 4: DAY 1

GERM to ESPINGO

DISTANCE:	11 miles	(17.7km)
ASCENT:	5320ft	(1620m)
DESCENT:	3258ft	(992m)

	Timings					
	Sect.	Accum.	Shop	Bar/ Café	Restau- rant	Accomm- odation
GERM			-	-	-	G/Y
PAS DE COURET	2.50	2.50	-	-	-	-
GRANGES D'ASTAU	2.25	5.15	-	+	-	G
LAC D'OO	1.10	6.25	-	-	-	R
COL D'ESPINGO	1.20	7.45	-	-	-	-
REFUGE D'ESPINGO	.5	7.50	-	-	-	R

The next two days to Luchon traverse some high and spectacular country. There are no villages but there are a number of refuges where meals may be purchased.

Leave Germ heading to the south and climb for a short while; cross a stream and follow a clear path that skirts and gradually climbs the hillside. This turns first to the south-west, then to the south before finally heading south-east. Follow the path to the Cabane d'Ourtiga (seen on the other side of the river). Here the route turns slightly to the left to climb more steeply. This gradient is maintained all the way to the Pas de Couret at 6999ft (2131m), the border between the Hautes

Pyrénées and the Haute Garonne.

Descend to the east on an obvious path. This passes a shepherd's hut and continues to descend steeply down the Val d'Esquierry. After nearly 2000 feet of descent the route enters forest and continues to descend until a roadhead is reached at the Granges d'Astau (gîte d'étape). Here turn south, pass the grange and refreshment bar and join a good track. Follow this as it climbs through woodland, negotiating numerous zig-zags, to the dam at the Lac d'Oô. This large mountain lake sports an impressive waterfall. There is a refuge here at the northern end of the lake (Auberge, Refuge du Lac d'Oô).

To continue on the GR 10 climb above the lake on a clear, well laid path with good views down to the lake on the right. The path slowly pulls away from the lake until a large boulder is reached where there is a sign indicating Luchon (6hrs 30mins). Turn sharp left here to continue on the GR 10, but if staying at the Refuge d'Espingo continue climbing south on a good path for about 10 minutes to reach the Col d'Espingo. The refuge is a few minutes walk from here and is situated in impressive surroundings at 6460ft (1967m).

SECTION 4: DAY 2

ESPINGO to LUCHON

DISTANCE:	11.2 miles	(18km)
ASCENT:	1681ft	(512m)
DESCENT:	6007ft	(1829m)

	Timings					
	Sect.	Accum.	Shop	Bar/ Café	Restau- rant	Accomm- odation
REFUGE D'ESPINGO			-	-	-	R
HOURQUETTE DES HOUNTS-SECS	1.15	1.15	-	-	-	-
COL DE LA COUME DE BOURG	1.10	2.25	-	-	-	-
SUPERBAGNERES	1.40	4.05	+	+	+	H+
BAGNERES-DE-LUCHON	2.40	6.45	++	++	++	H+. CP+

The first part of this section to Superbagnères offers superb high-level walking in magnificent surroundings. The descent is very long and tiring; one of the longest continuous descents on the GR 10.

Return to the large waymarked boulder to pick up the route of the GR 10. The route is always obvious until Superbagnères. The path is level for a while before climbing by a series of zig-zags to the Hourquette des Hounts-Secs at 7471ft (2275m). Superb views. Follow the clearly defined path heading generally in a north-easterly direction across the mountainside. Descend and reascend, crossing the north ridge of the Pic de Coume Nère. Descend and reascend a few zig-zags to reach the Col de la Coume de Bourg (7462ft;2272m).

Descend at first towards the south-east, but soon turning to head north-east again, cutting across steep, grassy slopes to arrive at the winter ski-complex of Superbagnères (5925ft;1804m). Here there are cafés and shops and multi-storied hotels. The area is still being developed and the numerous building projects and bulldozed tracks make navigation difficult. It is all too easy to take a track down to the hamlet of Gourron, after which there is no alternative but to follow a long winding road to Saint Aventin and then take the main road down into Luchon. Avoid this error at all costs. On arrival at Superbagnères follow the red / white waymarks down a steep ski piste, keeping close to the ski-lifts. Below this follow the waymarks carefully through woodland (NB do not follow the wooden sign marked 'Gourron, Luchon' down a steep forest track). If in doubt never walk far without the reassuring red / white waymarks. [Note: a later walker discovered that if the route is lost and Gourron is reached, a pleasant (but probably slightly longer) route can now be followed down through the woods to Luchon. It is waymarked with yellow circles containing the number 5.] The GR 10 descends into the valley to enter Luchon on the Superbagnères road close to a market.

Bagnères-de-Luchon (or simply Luchon as it is generally known) is the largest town since Saint-Jean-Pied-de-Port back in Basque country, and indeed no other town of comparable size will be met on the remainder of the GR 10 to the Mediterranean. It is the psychological, if not exactly the physical half-way point on the GR 10. It possesses a railway station with direct daily train services to Paris and it is therefore an ideal place to terminate or commence a section of the GR 10. There are a range of hotels and also many shops and supermarkets to chose from for replenishing food supplies. It is also one of the few places en route where there are banks for changing money or travellers cheques. (Note: it has been reported that the BNP Bank in Luchon will not accept Eurocheques.)

SECTION 4: DAY 3

LUCHON to FOS

DISTANCE:	18½ miles	(29.8km)
ASCENT:	5015ft	(1538m)
DESCENT:	5399ft	(1644m)

	Timings					
	Sect.	Accum.	Shop	Bar/ Café	Restau- rant	Accomm- odation
BAGNERES-DE-LUCHON			++	++	++	H+. CP+
SODE	1.25	1.25	-	-	-	-
ARTIGUE	.50	2.15	-	-	-	-
CABANE DE SAUNERES	1.15	3.30	-	-	-	C
CRETE DE CIGALERES	2.45	6.15	-	-	-	-
CABANES DES COURRAUS	.50	7.05	-	-	-	C
FOS	2.30	9.35	++	+	+	G. H.

West of Luchon the Pyrenees are bisected by the wide and deep Val d'Aran where the River Garonne runs down from Spain into France. The Franco-Spanish border makes a large detour to the north in this area and so the GR 10, always on French territory, traverses the mountains north-east of Luchon to the border town of Fos before turning to the east again to enter the Ariège. This stage passes through the picturesque villages of Sode and Artigue, before crossing the mountains and following the border for a while. The scenery here is excellent with views over to the high mountains of the main massif further south.

From the centre of Luchon find the Place du Comminges. From here follow the Avenue Maréchal-Foch and the Avenue de Toulouse heading north and passing to the rear of the railway station. Take the right turn on the road to Juzet-de-Luchon. Alternatively reach Juzet-de-Luchon via Lac Bades and along the river. This track, well waymarked, is the one to the east of the aerodrome marked on the IGN map. Cross over the bridge and walk right through the village to

Above the clouds, above Artigue

pick up and follow a path leading off from the right-hand side of the road. This waymarked route crosses the road (the D 46) several times and eventually joins it to enter the village of Sode. Follow the GR 10 signs to the rear of the church and climb the field beyond to find a narrow path in the trees (do not take the wide zig-zags leading up the field to the right). Climb the narrow path through woodland to the road (the D 46 again). Turn left and continue on the road to the village of Artigue (4040ft;1230m). There is a public telephone box in the village and a first-rate, inexpensive restaurant (closed on Mondays).

Take the track at the back of the church heading north-east. Follow this clear track all the way to the Cabane de Saunères at 5452ft (1660m). This cabane provides simple accommodation for up to three people and a wide panorama of the mountains of Luchon. The cabane has a fireplace and there is a water supply some 10 minutes walk to the east. At the cabane turn left and follow the signs uphill. Continue in a north-easterly direction all the way to the Plan de Montmajou (6338ft;1930m) where there are the two Cabanes de Peirahitta. After this the way becomes rather indistinct as it follows the Franco-Spanish border for a couple of miles. If in doubt keep to the crest and follow the line of small border posts. These are short, stubby concrete posts marked with symbols such as F 397 E. They are to be found at the tops of the hills forming the international frontier at this point. This part of the journey would be very difficult to negotiate in mist, and in bad weather it would be better to follow the alternative route that avoids the ridges (marked on the 1:50,000 IGN map). Follow the Crête de la Cigalères to the Col Aou (not marked on the 1:50,000 IGN map but situated between the Pic de Burat and the Pic de la Hage).

From the col descend steeply to the north, but after about 300 yards bear to the right (east) towards the tarn of Saint-Béat. Skirt round the lake and then head north to the two Cabanes des Courraus at 5209ft (1586m). One of these could possibly be used as an overnight refuge. Descend from here in a south-easterly direction and follow the path down through woodland, after a while turning to the north-east. At one point the path emerges onto a track, but after 100 yards or so on this you leave it on the right to continue the descent. Eventually, after a long descent, you emerge on the N 125 main road and turn right to walk into Fos (1787ft;544m). Note: a warning is given that the last part of the descent into Fos is awkward and slippery, particularly after rain. Care is needed. Here there is a gîte d'étape, a hotel, restaurant and two shops. It is advisable to purchase food supplies here as it is many days before the next shop is reached.

SECTION 4: DAY 4

FOS to ETANG D'ARAING

DISTANCE:	11 1/2 miles	(18.5km)
ASCENT:	5603ft	(1706m)
DESCENT:	985ft	(300m)

	Timings					
	Sect.	Accum.	Shop	Bar/ Café	Restau- rant	Accomm- odation
FOS			++	+	+	G. H.
MELLES	.45	.45	+	+	R	H
LABACH	1.15	2.00	-	-	-	-
CABANE D'ULS	2.20	4.20	-	-	-	C
PAS DU BOUC	1.15	5.35	-	-	-	-
COL D'AUERAN	.25	6.00	-	-	-	-
ETANG D'ARAING	.40	6.40	-	-	-	R

A long climb to the Col d'Auéran, but grand scenery. Walk through Fos on the N 125 heading towards the Spanish border. Turn left on the D 44 to ascend on this minor road to Melles. Walk through the village and continue on the road heading east and climbing numerous zig-zags to the hamlet of Labach-de-Melles (3218ft;980m). There is a water tap here but little else. Follow the waymarks through Labach then at the end of the road follow the path that climbs steeply through woodland. Several streams are passed before the route emerges from the trees and climbs steeply by a series of zig-zags to gain a high-level plateau. A little further is the small refuge of the Cabane d'Uls at 6135ft (1868m). This is owned by the Randonnées Pyrénéennes organisation and has space for about eight people. There is no electricity, but the hut has a fireplace, table, benches and bunk-beds (no mattresses).

From the refuge head south-east and climb steeply, following waymarks to a second high-level plateau. Cross this (grassland, but marshy in places) and then ascend to the Pas du Bouc (7127ft;2170m). Continue south-east on the obvious level path to the Col d'Auéran (7146ft;2176m). (If time is in hand and the day is fine, then a detour along the path heading south to the Pic de Crabère (8634ft;2629m) can be recommended. Return to the Col d'Aueran by the same route.) At the Col bear left (north-east and then east) and leave the province of the Haute Garonne to enter the Ariège. The route remains in this département for almost two weeks' walking. Head for the lake (Etang d'Araing) and refuge below. Descend on the waymarked path to the Refuge de l'Etang d'Araing (6404ft;1950m). This is a CAF refuge made from prefabricated metal sheets. There is room for forty-five people and meals are provided by the warden (resident in summer only).

The Refuge de l'Etang d'Araing is also the starting point for the five-day Tour du Biros. The waymarked path heads north from here on a large circuit to rejoin the GR 10 east of Grauillès.

SECTION 5: *THE ARIEGE*

INTRODUCTION

The département of the Ariège is a large and depopulated area of the Pyrenees. The depopulation of the region began in the mid-nineteenth century and today the main towns of Saint-Girons and Foix have only half the population they held in the 1850's. The rural areas have suffered even more during the last hundred years. Mining for iron, lead, zinc and other minerals has declined over the years and this has led to many people leaving the area for the large towns and cities to the north of the Pyrenees. The hamlets and small villages of the Ariège are today populated on the whole by elderly people.

The Ariège is quite an isolated part of Europe. A brief examination of the map will show that there is not a road pass over the mountains from France to Spain between the Col d'Aran (N 125) in the west and the Ariège valley (N 20) in the east. This is a huge area involving some two weeks of walking. The many French valleys are cul-de-sacs and this isolation has obviously contributed towards the economic decline and depopulation of the Ariège.

The western half of the region is known as the Couserans and is often referred to as the 'land of the eighteen valleys'. These valleys generally run in a north-south direction, and as the GR 10 basically travels west to east it follows that the route involves considerable amounts of ascent and descent. Despite this the path rarely goes above the 2000m (6568ft) mark and the way is less likely to be blocked by snow during the summer months than it often is in some of the regions to the west and east of the Ariège.

The difficulties of the Ariège are really related to its remoteness. It is perhaps less frequently traversed than the other sections of the GR 10 and consequently paths are often somewhat indistinct or difficult to follow. However in the summer of 1987 several parties of volunteers re-waymarked the GR 10 through some of the more difficult areas and it should therefore be easier to negotiate now. Several sections of the GR 10 through the Ariège have also been re-routed in recent years, which can also lead to difficulties if one picks up old markings. Several alterations to the GR 10 and the various options available are described in the text.

The Ariège is the only region through which the GR 10 passes where overnight accommodation and food provisioning can be a real problem. The predicament is alleviated somewhat by the presence of numerous cabanes where overnight shelter may be obtained, but the closing of several épiceries in the villages and the increasing use of mobile shops has increased the difficulties for the walker. The problems are expected to ease somewhat as time goes by as more gîtes d'étape are opened, so the GR 10 wayfarer should keep an eye open as he/she walks through the area for news of any new gîtes d'étape and refuges.

The number of tourists and hikers in the Ariège varies considerably with the time of year. The author walked alone through the region one September and at times had the impression that he was the only person left alive on earth! Even Europe has its wildernesses. However, the following July he encountered many other walkers on the GR 10 in the Couserans.

The Ariège, then, is a region for solitude and natural beauty. Many woods, lakes and mountain streams will be passed, and several wide grassy cols and upland plateaus traversed. Mention should be made of the little Lac de Bethmale, an idyllic spot surrounded by attractrive beech woodland. The most significant peak in the Couserans is Mont Valier (9320ft;2838m) which can be climbed by a detour from the GR 10. From this summit the Pic d'Estats and the Spanish mountains of the Encantados are visible.

The GR 10 passes through the Salat valley at Couflens, then continues over to the Ustou valley before reaching the small spa resort of Aulus-les-Bains. From here a highly scenic but often tortuous route leads over many remote cols and valleys north of Andorra before finally dropping down to the Ariège valley at Mérens-les-Vals. A train may be taken here, either south into Spain or up the Ariège valley with its extensive cave systems to Ax-les-Thermes, a well known spa town with good rail connections. The road south from Mérens-les-Vals leads into Andorra via the Port d'Envalira (in fact it is the only road route into Andorra from France). The mountains of Andorra are also well worth a visit, but alas the principality is better known as a haven for the duty-free shopper!

There have been a number of changes in the region of the Ariège through which the GR 10 passes since this guidebook was originally researched in the late 1980s, such that walkers may now prefer to make

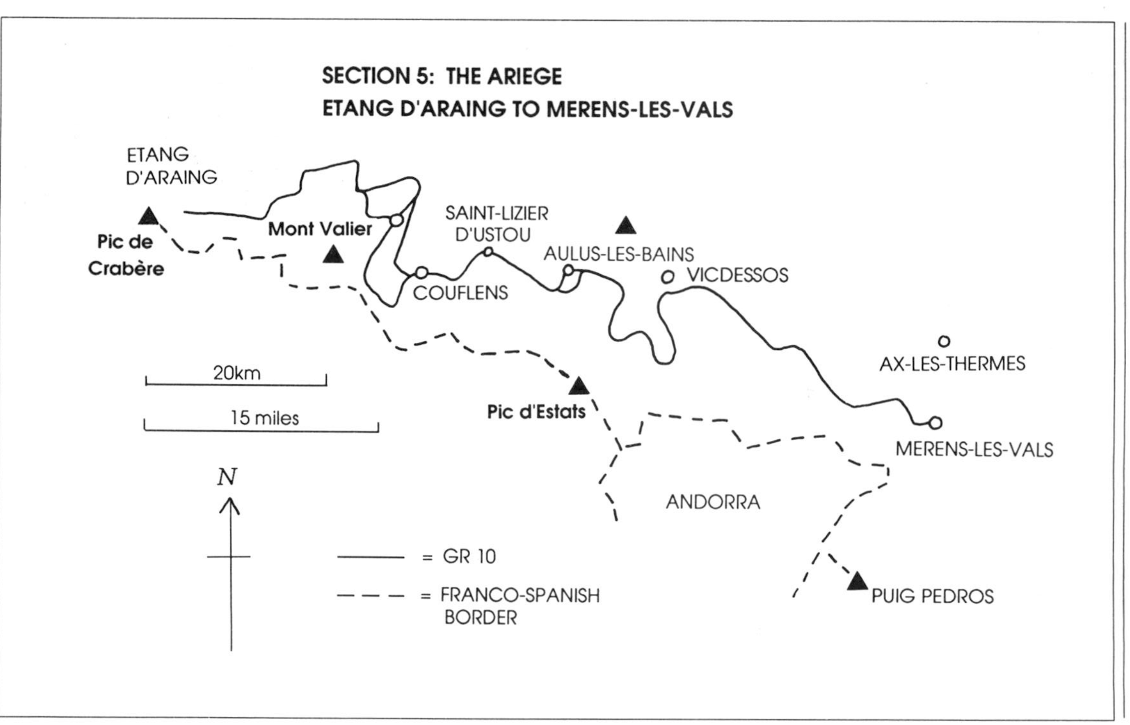
SECTION 5: THE ARIEGE
ETANG D'ARAING TO MERENS-LES-VALS
ETANG D'ARAING
Pic de Crabère
Mont Valier
SAINT-LIZIER D'USTOU
COUFLENS
AULUS-LES-BAINS
VICDESSOS
AX-LES-THERMES
Pic d'Estats
MERENS-LES-VALS
ANDORRA
PUIG PEDROS
20km
15 miles
N
= GR 10
= FRANCO-SPANISH BORDER

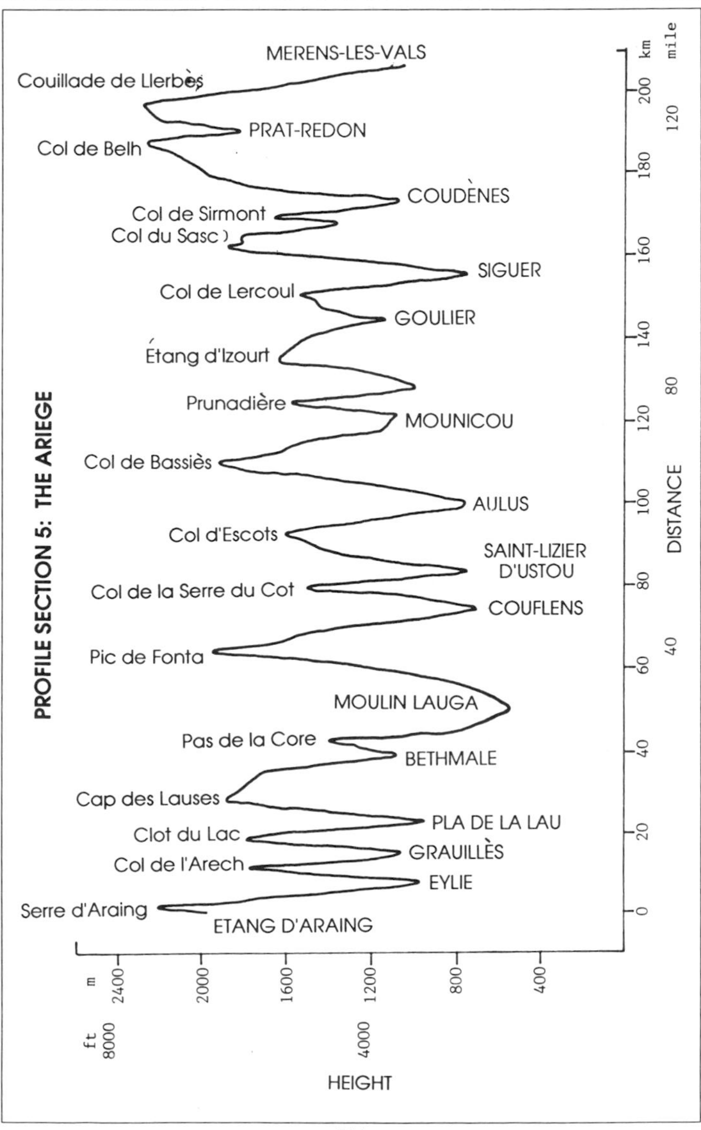
PROFILE SECTION 5: THE ARIEGE
MERENS-LES-VALS
Couillade de Llerbès
PRAT-REDON
Col de Belh
COUDÈNES
Col de Sirmont
Col du Sasc
SIGUER
Col de Lercoul
GOULIER
Étang d'Izourt
Prunadière
MOUNICOU
Col de Bassiès
AULUS
Col d'Escots
SAINT-LIZIER D'USTOU
Col de la Serre du Cot
COUFLENS
Pic de Fonta
MOULIN LAUGA
Pas de la Core
BETHMALE
Cap des Lauses
PLA DE LA LAU
Clot du Lac
GRAUILLÈS
Col de l'Arech
EYLIE
Serre d'Araing
ETANG D'ARAING
km
mile
0
20
40
60
80
100
120
140
160
180
200
40
80
120
DISTANCE
m
2400
2000
1600
1200
800
400
ft
8000
4000
HEIGHT

some alteration to the stages proposed in this book. Various updated notes have been made in the text below to help the walker make logistical route planning decisions. Considering the worsening accommodation problems in the Ariége, it is strongly recommended that a tent is carried through this region.

SECTION 5: DAY 1

ETANG D'ARAING to GRAUILLES

DISTANCE:	9 miles	(14.5km)
ASCENT:	3882ft	(1182m)
DESCENT:	6509ft	(1982m)

	Timings Sect.	Accum.	Shop	Bar/ Café	Restau- rant	Accomm- odation
ETANG D'ARAING			-	-	-	R
SERRE D'ARAING	.50	.50	-	-	-	-
EYLIE	3.00	3.50	-	-	-	G
COL DE L'ARECH	2.45	6.35	-	-	-	-
PASSERELLE DE GRAUILLES	1.30	8.05	-	-	-	-
CABANE DE GRAUILLES	.05	8.10	-	-	-	C

The first full day in the Ariège and the remoteness of the area and lack of facilities soon become evident. There is a good gîte d'étape at the small hamlet of Eylie at the half-way stage. If the weather is uncertain it would be wise to stay at the gîte rather than continuing into fairly remote country. There are no shops en route, but it may be possible to buy provisions at Estoéou or if not, then certainly at Sentein further down the Biros valley. There are also hotels, a campsite and a bus to Saint-Girons from Sentein.

From the Refuge de l'Etang d'Araing descend to the far end of the lake to skirt the newly constructed dam. Climb up the hill behind the dam, heading to the south-east until the Serre d'Araing is reached at 7294ft (2221m). It may give some brief satisfaction after this stiff pull to realise that this is the last time that the GR 10 ventures above the 2000m mark until the Col de la Didorte on the approach to Mérens-les-Vals. Begin the long descent into the Biros Valley. From the Serre d'Araing first bear right to descend over an area of slate and then follow the obvious and well waymarked paths to pass several disused lead and zinc mine workings. Pass a plaque dedicated to some of the pioneers of the electrical industry in France. Eventually descend through woodland to emerge at the gîte d'étape at Eylie. Note the rather disheartening signpost giving walking times to places further east. An overnight stop at this gîte can be recommended (excellent food, hospitality and the possibility of purchasing basic provisions from the guardian).

From the gîte follow the path round to the right to cross the river at 3153ft (960m). Turn left for a few yards before striking out right to ascend the very steep hillside up to some zig-zags. These lead up to a gate. (Note: about 10 minutes above this gate is a water source. It is located underneath a flat rock on the track which carries a waymark and the running water can be heard on the approach.) Pass through this and continue upwards through heather, bilberry and some woodland. Eventually reach the grassy Col de l'Arech at 5918ft (1802m). From here head south-east taking care to follow the sparse red/white waymarks leading down to a dirt track. There is a small cabane in this region (Cabane de l'Arech, 5379ft;1638m) which would give shelter for about four people and which has a water source nearby. Follow the track downhill for about 10 minutes until, at a bend, you take a narrow path through heather and bilberry. This descends steeply to enter woodland. Follow the pleasant path through the trees until a small bridge is seen crossing the river over to the left.

Descend to this bridge (the Passerelle de Grauillès). The GR 10 passes over this bridge, but for the cabane continue on up the left bank of the river for about 350 yards without crossing the bridge. The Cabane de Grauillès is situated at 3777ft (1150m) in a lonely but beautiful area, the mountains towards the border to the south creating an impressive setting. The cabane sleeps about two to three people on a hard wooden sleeping area (room for about eight other people upstairs). There is a table and a fireplace. Water is available from the nearby river. An alternative to stopping at the Cabane de Grauilles is the Cabane de Besset (see below). It is beatuifully situated and was completely renovated in 1995.

SECTION 5: DAY 2

GRAUILLES to CABANE DU TAUS

DISTANCE:	9 miles	(14.5km)
ASCENT:	5912ft	(1800m)
DESCENT:	3307ft	(1007m)

	Timings Sect.	Accum.	Shop	Bar/ Café	Restau- rant	Accomm- odation
CABANE DE GRAUILLES			-	-	-	C
CABANE DE BESSET	1.35	1.35	-	-	-	C
CLOT DU LAC	1.00	2.35	-	-	-	C
PLA DE LA LAU	2.20	4.55	-	-	-	C
PASSERELLES DES GARDES	.10	5.05	-	-	-	-
CABANE DU TAUS	2.50	7.55	-	-	-	C

A glance at the above table will give a good indication of the remoteness of this country. No places of permanent human habitation are passed on this route, although a motorable road is crossed at the Pla de la Lau. There are no shops, no places where refreshment may be bought and the only accommodation is that to be found in unguarded cabanes. Obviously all food will have to be carried, as well as the means to cook it, unless lengthy detours from the route are envisaged. Apart from the remoteness of the area and the strenuous nature of the route, there should be few other problems during normal conditions as the path is mainly over grassy or wooded hillsides.

From the Cabane de Grauillès return to the bridge to cross the river. Follow the waymarked path to a signpost indicating the way to the Pla de la Lau. Climb steeply out of the Vallée d'Orle mainly through woodland and often following a series of zig-zags. Emerge from the trees at the Cabane de Besset at 4907ft (1494m). This sleeps about five people and has a fireplace. Water can be found about 300 yards to the south on a level path. Continue the climb to reach the highest point at the Clot du Lac at 5980ft (1821m). Here there is another cabane offering the usual hard, wooden sleeping area.

From the Clot du Lac begin a long, tedious descent, first in a south-easterly direction but later turning to head in a northerly one. There are many paths in this area and care is required to follow only the red/white signs. Before entering woodland the GR 10 passes close to yet another small cabane. Follow the waymarked path down through the trees to reach a dirt track at the Pla de la Lau (3044ft;927m). Two small cabanes can also be found here, each sleeping about four people.

Turn right on the dirt track and follow this for a short way before descending to the river (look out for GR 10 signs on a tree to the left of the dirt track). Cross the bridge and follow the waymarks through the trees. Soon bear off to the left to climb steeply through woodland (to climb Mont Valier do not turn left here but continue ahead to a second bridge from where a waymarked route is followed to the summit). Climb the zig-zags through this woodland, at times alongside a gushing river. Emerge from the trees to continue upwards past the point where the Cabane d'Aouen used to stand (it was destroyed by avalanche in the mid-1990s). Proceed up the hillside on a series of zig-zags. The path is well waymarked. Nearing the top of the climb at the Cap des Lauses the GR 10 veers to the left (north-west) but instead now head south for about 10 minutes to locate the Cabane du Taus which sleeps about 5 people.

SECTION 5: DAY 3

CABANE DU TAUS to ESBINTS

DISTANCE:	10miles	(16.1km)
ASCENT:	1251ft	(381m)
DESCENT:	4972ft	(1514m)

	Timings Sect.	Accum.	Shop	Bar/ Café	Restau- rant	Accomm- odation
CABANE DU TAUS			-	-	-	C
CAP DES LAUSES	.10	.10	-	-	-	-
COL DE LA LAZIES	.45	1.55	-	-	-	-
COL D'AUEDOLE	1.20	2.15	-	-	-	-
ETANG DE BETHMALE	1.40	3.55	-	-	-	-
PAS DE LA CORE	1.40	5.35	-	-	-	-
ESBINTS	1.20	6.55	-	-	-	-

The GR 10 continues through remote country. However, civilisation may be encountered when the route emerges on the D 17 road at the Pas de la Core. As with yesterday's route there are several streams and rivers from which water may be obtained.

From the Cabane du Taus return to the Cap des Lauses and then head north-west to follow an undulating high level route. At the Col de la Laziès (6043ft;1840m) turn towards the east to enter the area of country known as Bethmale. Continue on the waymarked route to descend to a small mountain lake (Etang d'Ayes) and climb again to reach the Col d'Auédole at 5682ft (1730m). There is a variant route from here to the Pas de la Core which is shorter than the standard route. It was the old GR 10 route (now referred to as the GR 10 D) and is marked on the 1:50,000 IGN map, leaving the Col d'Auédole in an easterly direction.

The new route of the GR 10 goes to the Pas de la Core via the picturesque Etang de Bethmale. From the Col d'Auédole drop down to the north-east to pass a small hut with corrugated-metal roof. This is used for animals and is not suitable for sleeping. Follow the waymarks down from here, soon entering woodland. Join a forest track and remain on this for some time to approach the Granges du Mont Noir. Leave the track on a well marked path which contours through trees changing direction several times. Descend to the lake (Etang de Bethmale) and carry on following the line of the road. Eventually the path comes out at this road (the D 17). Turn right at the road for about a quarter of a mile before leaving it on the right to climb on a zig-zagging path to emerge once more on the road at the Pas de la Core (4581ft;1395m). (A semi-permanent refreshment caravan may be here, serving sandwiches, snacks and drinks.)

There are two routes from the Pas de la Core. If the gîte d'étape at Esbints is not required then take the GR 10 D variant to Estours (see below). For Esbints follow the new GR 10 route down the valley in an easterly direction. The route is well waymarked and follows a forest track and a footpath to pass the Cabane de Tariolle, then continues on to Artigue d'Esbints. Follow a line of ash trees and pass in front of another shepherd's cabane. Continue down the valley following the course of the river to the hamlet of Esbints (2660ft;810m). N.B. The gîte d'étape that was located here was burnt down in the mid 1990s, but the shepherd's wife in the hamlet offers accommodation.

Alternatively, there is a new gîte d'étape (opened 1995) at Aunac, 2 miles south-east of Esbints, on the way to Moulin Lauga.

GR 10 D Variant from the **PAS de la CORE to ESTOURS**

DISTANCE:	$7^{1/2}$miles	(12.1km)
ASCENT:	604ft	(184m)
DESCENT:	2969ft	(904m)

	Timings Sect.	Accum.	Shop	Bar/ Café	Restau- rant	Accomm- odation
PAS DE LA CORE			-	-	-	-
LUZURS	.40	.40	-	-	-	C
COL DU SOULARIL	.50	1.30	-	-	-	-
SUBERA	.35	2.05	-	-	-	C
LAMEZA	.20	2.25	-	-	-	C
ESTOURS	1.50	4.15	-	-	-	-

This was the old GR 10 route and is marked on the IGN 1:50,000 map. The red/white markings are still present, but are often faded and difficult to follow. However the way should rarely be in doubt.

At the Pas de la Core take a level path that follows the road for a little way before heading into woodland. Emerge from this just above and to the right of the Cabane de Lazurs (no water here). Climb on a well marked path which then levels out and skirts the mountainside to arrive at Casabède. Continue past this to the Col du Soularil (5186ft;1579m). Descend from here first in a south-westerly direction to the Cabane de Subera. Here change direction to head to the north-east down the valley. On reaching the small Cabane de Lameza turn off left into the woodland and descend with the cascading stream on the left (care!). On emerging at the Grange d'Arros, cross over the river to find an overgrown path which follows it down the valley all the way to a bridge. Cross the river again by this bridge to reach a dirt track which re-joins the new GR 10 in the vicinity of Estours. Turn left for Moulin Lauga or right to continue on the new GR 10 route to Couflens.

SECTION 5: DAY 4

ESBINTS to CABANE D'AULA

DISTANCE:	10.6 miles	(17.1km)
ASCENT:	3314ft	(1009m)
DESCENT:	883ft	(269m)

	Timings					
	Sect.	Accum.	Shop	Bar/ Café	Restau- rant	Accomm- odation
ESBINTS			-	-	-	-
PONT DU SALAT	1.10	1.10	-	-	-	-
MOULIN LAUGA	.15	1.25	-	-	(+)	(H)
ESTOURS	.50	2.15	-	-	-	-
CABANE D'AULA	2.45	5.00	-	-	-	C

Accommodation and food supply problems are still present. It would be possible for strong walkers to reach the gîte d'étape at Rouse in one day, although this would be a long, hard march. However the following day to Saint Lizier d'Ustou would then be quite short. The other alternative is to break the journey in two, as described here, by stopping at a mountain cabane. There are still no shops en route from which to buy provisions, but a 1.5 mile (2.4km) walk on the road to the north from the Pont du Salat will lead to Seix, where there are shops, hotels, restaurants and buses to Saint-Girons.

The route to Couflens via the Col de Pause is relatively new. Until a few years ago the GR 10 went from Moulin Lauga over the Pic de Fonta and so down to Couflens. The route is still possible although care in navigation is required, particularly on descent. Old red / white markings can still be seen in places. There is a particularly fine view from the summit. A route description for this shorter, but harder variant is given after the description of the standard route.

From the gîte d'étape at Esbints continue in an easterly direction, soon taking a right fork to follow a clear footpath close to the river. Cross the stream by a bridge, pass through an area of woodland and arrive at a road. Turn right and about 300 yards later turn left off the road to the Camp de Peyrot. Continue to the hamlet of Aunac. From here descend to the south-east down the Coume-Chaude valley to reach a bridge over the river (Pont du Salat). Turn left here for the numerous facilities that Seix has to offer, but if continuing on the GR 10 turn right and continue to the village of Moulin Lauga (1777ft;541m). There is a hotel-restaurant at the Pont de la Taule, about 1 mile along the D 3 road in a south-easterly direction.

Leave Moulin Lauga to the west to follow a track which soon turns to the south-west to follow the River Estours. Pass the point where the River Arros joins the Estours (ie where the GR 10 D variant rejoins the GR 10) and continue up the Estours valley heading south-west. Pass the Cabane de l'Artigue at 3458ft (1053m). This is normally closed. Continue the ascent to pass the Torrent de l'Artigue and negotiate a series of zig-zags in woodland to reach the Cabane d'Aula (5090ft;1550m). This has room for about twelve people. There is a fireplace and a source of water.

MOULIN LAUGA to COUFLENS via PIC de FONTA

DISTANCE:	9.6 miles	(15.5km)
ASCENT:	4562ft	(1389m)
DESCENT:	4043ft	(1231m)

	Timings Sect.	Timings Accum.	Shop	Bar/ Café	Restau- rant	Accomm- odation
MOULIN LAUGA			-	-	(+)	(H)
SAHUSSET	.35	.35	-	-	-	-
PIC DE FONTA	3.15	3.50	-	-	-	-
LASSERRE	1.40	5.30	-	-	-	-
COUFLENS	.50	6.20	-	-	+	H*

* There is a gîte d'étape at Rouze (see Section 5, Day 5 p120).

Take the path adjacent to the small bridge in Moulin Lauga. This clearly defined route leads to the picturesque hamlet of Sahusset (2568ft;782m) where water may be obtained. From here take a zig-zagging path through trees. Climb on a poorly waymarked path through woodland generally heading in a south-westerly direction. On emerging from the trees continue upwards, bearing to the left to gain the ridge ascending to the Pic de Fonta. This becomes rough underfoot with heather and grass and an abundance of raspberry bushes. Attain the summit of the Pic de Fonta (6348ft;1933m) where there is a wide panorama. Mont Valier is particularly noticeable.

Head downhill across heather and grass. There is no path and no waymarkings. Head at first to the east-south-east, but on approaching trees do not enter the wood. Instead keep to the right of the trees and descend to a wide grassy plateau at 4269ft (1300m). Traverse this area in a southerly direction to pick up occasional red / white faded marks on trees. Eventually reach the Granges de Lasserre and the D 703. Turn left on this road and continue to the bridge at Couflens (or follow the route as described under Section 5, Day 5).

SECTION 5: DAY 5

CABANE D'AULA to SAINT-LIZIER D'USTOU

DISTANCE:	13 miles	(20.9km)
ASCENT:	4250ft	(1294m)
DESCENT:	6910ft	(2104m)

	Timings					
	Sect.	Accum.	Shop	Bar/ Café	Restau- rant	Accomm- odation
CABANE D'AULA			-	-	-	C
ETANG D'ARREAU	1.30	1.30	-	-	-	-
COL DE PAUSE	1.10	2.40	-	-	-	-
COUFLENS	1.40	4.20	-	-	-	-
ROUZE	.45	5.05	-	-	-	G
COL DE LA SERRE DU COT	1.10	6.15	-	-	-	-
SAINT-LIZIER D'USTOU	1.40	7.55	+	+	-	CP

Two climbs today, in an area still lacking in facilities. There used to be an épicerie in Couflens but it is now necessary to climb over into the next valley for the first shop to be encountered on the GR 10 since Fos, 6 days ago. There is a gîte d'étape at the hamlet of Rouze and so a short day could finish here, still allowing sufficient time to reach Aulus on the following day.

From the Cabane d'Aula climb towards the south-east, negotiating a zig-zagging route. Later veer towards the east to pass a col and then descend to the Etang d'Arreau. Continue the descent to a shepherd's

In the vicinity of Couflens

hut, the Cabane d'Arreau (5570ft;1696m), closed. Descend to a road (D 703) and stay on this for about half a mile before leaving it on the left to follow waymarks to the Col de Pause (5015ft;1527m). From here the route follows the general direction of the road, leaving it at times to take short cuts but always re-joining it. Pass the Granges de Lasserre where the variant from the Pic de Fonta joins the main route. After Faup make for Raufaste, then walk the level path to Casteras. Descend again to Angouls and from here take a road into Couflens (2305ft; 702m), where there is a telephone. The village has lost most of its facilities over the last few years and now is only served by a mobile shop.

From the centre of Couflens follow the D 3 road to the bridge at the north end of the village. Here follow a red / white waymarked path heading gently uphill, following the right bank of a river to reach the hamlet of Rouze where there is a gîte d'étape (recommended: good meals). Continue with the gîte on the right to climb past ruined buildings. The route is fairly obvious, ascending mainly through woodland. Eventually emerge from the trees to reach the Col de la Serre du Cot at 5077ft (1546m). There are a multitude of paths here, but continue over the pass maintaining direction to enter woodland once again after a few hundred yards. Descend through this woodland paying particular attention to the numerous path turnings which are poorly waymarked. (Note: waymarking was reported in 1996 to be much improved.) The way eventually becomes more obvious as it descends into the Ustou valley emerging at the road in the village of Saint-Lizier d'Ustou (2430ft;740m). Note that there is an alternative route from Couflens to Saint-Lizier d'Ustou via the Col des Portes (5911ft;1800m). This was the original route of the GR 10.

Saint-Lizier d'Ustou has a mini-supermarket and campsite. There used to be a gîte d'étape in the village but alas it has now closed. Either make use of the campsite or walk to Le Trein where there is a good hotel (Hôtel des Ombres).

SECTION 5: DAY 6

SAINT-LIZIER D'USTOU to AULUS-LES-BAINS

DISTANCE:	10.3 miles	(16.6km)
ASCENT:	3048ft	(928m)
DESCENT:	3015ft	(918m)

(These figures refer to the direct route.)

	Timings Sect.	Accum.	Shop	Bar/ Café	Restau- rant	Accomm- odation
SAINT-LIZIER D'USTOU			+	+	+	CP
PIC & COL DE FITTE	2.00	2.00	-	-	-	C
COL D'ESCOTS	.45	2.45	-	-	-	C
CIRQUE DE CASIERENS	.55	3.40	-	-	-	-
JASSE DE FOUILLET	.45	4.25	-	-	-	-
AULUS-LES-BAINS	1.00	5.25	++	++	++	G. H+
VARIANT						
JASSE DE FOUILLET			-	-	-	-
ETANG DE GUZET	.50	.50	-	-	-	-
PASSERELLE D'ARS	.50	1.40	-	-	-	-
AULUS-LES-BAINS	1.40	3.20	++	++	++	G. H+

Today's destination, Aulus-les-Bains, marks the mid-way point of the traverse of the Ariège and is the largest town since Luchon. Enjoy the facilities to be found in Aulus as there is no equivalent centre of civilisation until Mérens-les-Vals, a further week's walk along the GR 10.

There are two routes into Aulus from the Jasse de Fouillet. The direct route which requires no additional climbing is described first, followed by the more picturesque but much longer variant via the Etang de Guzet and the Passerelle d'Ars.

Walk south along the D 38 passing a telephone box, bench and shop on the right. At a small Roman bridge turn left and follow the red/ white waymarks through shaded woodland. Climb steadily, eventually emerging onto open hillside with good views of high mountains over to the right. Continue to the Pic and Col de Fitté (4555ft;1387m) where there is a small cabane. From here the ascent continues until a height of about 5420ft (1650m) is reached. A short gentle descent then leads to the Col d'Escots (5314ft;1618m) where there is another small cabane and a road which leads in about 40 minutes to the ski-resort of Guzet-Neige. Here there are hotels, a restaurant and a campsite. However, the GR 10 does not take this road but rather descends to the south-east over well-waymarked but rough ground to reach the river and the impressive Cirque de Casièrens. Cross the river and follow it downhill heading generally in a northerly direction. Pass a set of waterfalls (Les Cascades du Fouillet) and enter woodland. After a while pass a prominent sign indicating the descent to Aulus and the GR 10 to the Etang de Guzet (see below). For the direct route to Aulus-les-Bains continue in a northerly direction before swinging to the north-east to descend to the village. Cross the river and road and follow the signs to the gîte d'étape which is near to an old church, a little under half a mile from the river. The gîte d'étape in Aulus with its friendly and helpful guardian is recommended.

VARIANT

At the Jasse de Fouillet (3842ft;1170m) take the waymarked path to the right heading in a north-easterly direction. This leads to the Souliou plateau (4204ft;1280m) where the route changes direction, climbing towards the south-east through trees to reach the Etang de Guzet (4792ft;1459m). With the lake on the right continue climbing to reach some ruined cabanes. Heading first towards the south-east but soon veering to the east, follow a route (partly through forest) which eventually descends a zig-zag path to the Passerelle d'Ars (4877ft;1485m). Cross the bridge and follow the waymarked route, passing the Cascades d'Ars. Follow the river to reach a second bridge (Pont d'Atrigous, 3481ft;1060m). Continue down the valley to join a track. Follow this for over half a mile before leaving it to follow the river down to the Pont de la Mouline (2578ft;785m). Cross this bridge and in about 350 yards reach a road where you turn left for Aulus-les-Bains or right to continue on the GR 10.

SECTION 5: DAY 7

AULUS-LES-BAINS to MOUNICOU

DISTANCE:	13.8 miles	(22.2km)
ASCENT:	4345ft	(1323m)
DESCENT:	3235ft	(985m)

	Timings Sect.	Accum.	Shop	Bar/ Café	Restau- rant	Accomm- odation
AULUS-LES-BAINS			++	++	++	G. H+
COUMEBIERE	2.10	2.10	-	-	-	-
PORT DE SALEIX	1.20	3.30	-	-	-	-
COL DE BASSIES	.50	4.20	-	-	-	-
ETANG DE BASSIES	.40	5.00	-	-	-	-
ETANG D'ESCALES	.30	5.30	-	-	-	-
CHAPELLE DE SAINT ANTOINE	2.45	8.15	-	-	-	-
MOUNICOU	.25	8.40	-	+	-	G

A first rate section with impressive scenery. Remember to stock up with food before leaving Aulus-les-Bains. The charming gîte d'étape at Mounicou does not provide evening meals, although there are the usual self-catering facilities. The guardian also runs the adjacent café where breakfast is served. An alternative to continuing to Mounicou is to stop overnight at the relatively new CAF Refuge de Bassiès (guarded) marked on the latest IGN maps (recommended food and hospitality). It is situated at the NW end of the Lacs de Bessiès.

Follow the waymarks from the gîte d'étape at Aulus-les-Bains to the main road (D 3). Follow this east and then south-east, passing the route from the Cascades d'Ars on the right. After about three quarters of a mile on this road turn left at the red/white waymark. Climb on this path through woodland. This levels out somewhat after a while, but then continues more steeply, crossing several rivers to emerge from the trees at an open plateau and road (Coumebière,

From the Port de Saleix

4598ft;1400m). This is an attractive green plateau where wild horses roam.

Cross the road and continue in an easterly direction to climb a series of wide zig-zags up to the Port de Saleix (5892ft;1794m). From here there are extensive views down to the valley in the east. This is also the point from which the five-day Tour du Massif des Trois Seigneurs leaves the GR 10 route. The GR 10 climbs steeply for about 400ft (122m) from the Port de Saleix, heading towards the south. From the rocky crest descend to the Etang d'Alate. The red/white waymarkings are poor from here on. Aim in a south-easterly direction for the Col de Bassiès (6348ft;1933m) There is a superb panorama from here over to high snow-capped mountains.

Descend steeply from the col to the Pla de la Font. Follow a footpath over rocky undulating ground to pass to the left of three lakes (Etangs de Bassiès and the Etang d'Escales). About 150 yards after the last lake cross a small stone footbridge over the river and descend on a path in a south-easterly direction. This later turns towards the south to follow a route above the Auzat valley, eventually descending to the road at the bridge and chapel of Saint Antoine de Montcalm. From here take the old footpath on the right bank of the river (or alternatively the road on the opposite bank) to the hamlet of Mounicou, where the gîte d'étape will be found.

SECTION 5: DAY 8

MOUNICOU to GOULIER

DISTANCE:	14 miles	(22.5km)
ASCENT:	3905ft	(1189m)
DESCENT:	3829ft	(1166m)

	Timings					
	Sect.	Accum.	Shop	Bar/ Café	Restau- rant	Accomm- odation
MOUNICOU			-	+	-	G
REFUGE DE PRUNADIERE	1.40	1.40	-	-	-	-
ARTIES	1.50	3.30	-	-	-	-
BARRAGE DE L'ETANG D'IZOURT	2.20	5.50	-	-	-	(R)
GOULIER	2.30	8.20	-	+	+	G

The GR 10 passes through an attractive area amidst impressive scenery during the next two days, but those walkers with sights on the distant Mediterranean coast may feel somewhat frustrated, as little progress is made towards the east despite considerable effort! The route consists of three to four giant loops heading towards the Franco-Spanish frontier, but each time returning towards the wide French valley in the north in which the towns of Auzat and Vicdessos can be found. The first stage visits the high, dammed Etang d'Izourt before heading to the gîte d'étape at Goulier.

Cross the bridge at Mounicou and turn right on the road heading south. After about 150 yards turn left on a footpath (no red/white waymark at this point). Climb on a zig-zagging path walking near to the edge of a ravine at times. Eventually turn towards the north-north-east climbing gradually. Pass the Casteillous rocks and a little afterwards enter woodland to reach the Refuge de Prunadière (5301ft;1614m). There is a source of water here. Descend through the forest in a northerly direction on a well waymarked footpath. The path climbs again for a short distance to reach and cross a wooded ridge and descend once more. After a while the route turns to the south-east and commences a series of large zig-zags down through forest to reach a road and the hamlet of Artiès. If provisions are required at this stage they can be obtained at the town of Auzat which is reached in an hour by turning left at this road. Auzat has hotels, a campsite and several shops.

The GR 10, however, turns right on the road and follows it to the Centrale Electrique de Pradières. There is a new auberge / restaurant / café here where accommodation and meals are offered, although the establishment is often crowded with large groups. The auberge opened in 1992 to commemorate 20 years since the opening of the GR 10 in the Auzat valley. Continue on the same bearing, following the general direction of the river to climb gradually to the dam at the Etang d'Izourt (5409ft;1647m). There is a cabane here providing shelter for up to ten people. From here a route (the GR 10 A) may be taken along the east side of the lake and up to the Etang and Refuge du Fourcat at 8030ft(2445m). This refuge has a resident guardian during the summer, is on the HRP route and commands fine views of the mountains close to the Spanish border.

However the GR 10 heads north from the Etang d'Izourt. The route crosses a series of small streams and passes a little above the building of Coumasses-Grandes. Continue along the escarpment with fine views down to the valley below, passing above Artiès (there is a drinking water supply here). Enter woodland and reach a commemorative plinth at 4631ft (1410m). This commemorates the opening of the GR 10 through the Ariège in October 1975. It is also the starting point for another variant to the standard route, the GR 10 B which by-passes Goulier and rejoins the GR 10 at the Col de l'Esquérus. The standard route descends towards the north-east to meet and cross a road. The path descends to Goulier (3645ft;1110m) and the gîte d'étape and restaurant / bar. There is another gîte d'étape in the village, up the hill near the GR 10 departure point (Gîte d'Endron).

Walkers will have to take stock at Goulier as there is now no longer the possibility of buying provisions at Siguer. It is strongly advised to go to Vicdessos / Auzat to reprovision before proceeding (best done from Goulier [no shops]). Several walkers have reported that they found it easy to hitch lifts up and down the valley, the locals being aware of the situation.

SECTION 5: DAY 9

GOULIER to SIGUER

DISTANCE:	7 miles	(11.3km)
ASCENT:	1442ft	(439m)
DESCENT:	2657ft	(809m)

	Timings					
	Sect.	Accum.	Shop	Bar/ Café	Restau- rant	Accomm- odation
GOULIER			-	+	+	G
COL DE RISOUL	.40	.40	-	-	-	-
COL DE L'ESQUERUS	.45	1.25	-	-	-	-
COL DE GRAIL	.50	2.15	-	-	-	-
COL DE LERCOUL	.30	2.45	-	-	-	-
LERCOUL	.50	3.35	-	-	-	-
SIGUER	.50	4.25	-	-	-	G

Today's stage is short, but it is best not to go on past Siguer as there is no proper accommodation (and indeed no permanent habitation after Gestiès) for the following 4 days.

From Goulier take the old miners' track heading north-east to the Col de Risoul (4368ft;1330m). Leave the road and follow the ridge, eventually meeting the GR 10 variant coming in from the right, and climb to the Col de L'Esquérus. From here take the path leading to the south-east to walk across the upper end of the Sem valley, mainly in woodland, to arrive at the Col de Grail (4877ft;1485m).

Next climb towards the north. After a short while when the path divides, take the left branch and descend in the same direction, eventually reaching the Col de Lercoul at 5087ft (1549m) below the Pic de la Bède.

Take the path heading north-east from the Col de Lercoul to descend through the forest. The path veers towards the north. Cross a road and take a path into the old village of Lercoul, which is only inhabited during the summer months. Pass the church and take the road descending into the Siguer valley. After a little over half a mile, at a bend in the road, take a path off into the woods. This soon descends steeply, eventually joining the road just before Siguer. The café-

The Pic de Cubanatous from the Col de Bassiès

On the Crête des Isards

View from the Porteille de Bésines

The End! The beach at Banyuls-sur-Mer

The church at Siguer

épicere-auberge that was in the main street has now closed. There is dormitory style accommodation in the village: to locate this follow the sign "Acceuil Randonneurs" which is off the main street to the left, beyond where the GR 10 goes off to the left (note that this establishment offers neither food nor cooking facilities).

SECTION 5: DAY 10

SIGUER to REFUGE DE BALLEDREYT

DISTANCE:	6.2 miles	(10km)
ASCENT:	3994ft	(1216m)
DESCENT:	1169ft	(356m)

	Timings					
	Sect.	Accum.	Shop	Bar/ Café	Restau- rant	Accomm- odation
SIGUER			-	-	-	G
GESTIES	.35	.35	-	-	-	-
COL DE GAMEL	1.40	2.15	-	-	-	-
PLA DE MONTCAMP	2.00	4.15	-	-	-	-
COL DU SASC	.20	4.35	-	-	-	-
COURTAL MARTI	.40	5.15	-	-	-	-
REFUGE DE BALLEDREYT	.30	5.45	-	-	-	C

The eastern section of the Ariège from Siguer to Mérens-les-Vals passes through some of the wildest landscape on the whole of the GR 10. After leaving Gestiès, the small village above Siguer, there is no further permanent habitation until Mérens-les-Vals, a walk of 3-4 days. Few roads are passed and even those that are encountered are only minor ones, used by shepherds or built by the EDF (Electricité de France). The area is away from the major walking and mountaineering routes and so relatively few other walkers will be seen. Shepherds, farmers and anglers testing their skill on the numerous rivers may be encountered. The ability to use map and compass is essential in this near wilderness area. The red / white waymarking system tends to be rather poor in places, although officials with red and white paint pots did make some improvements during the summer of 1987. Clear waymarking would make a considerable difference on this section. Although the route does not cross any particularly steep or rocky areas, straying from a recognised route could have disastrous results. The distances may not seem great, but most people find the terrain tiring and time consuming. The area should not be underestimated.

Backpackers carrying their own tents will be at a distinct advantage on this section. There is no guarded accommodation available until Mérens-les-Vals is reached, the only form of shelter being the mountain cabanes. Fortunately there are several of these and they will be mentioned in the text. Remember that some of these may be locked and some could have been converted for animal use. Some new ones may have been erected (always consult the latest maps). Similarly there are no shops, cafés or restaurants until Mérens-les-Vals, so it is essential that sufficient food for 4 days is bought and carried from Siguer. Remember also that if the weather changes during a crossing it may be necessary to hole-up for a while in one of the cabanes.

The section from Siguer to Refuge de Clarans has been divided into 2 rather short days, stopping the first night at Balledreyt. Stronger walkers may wish to combine these 2 days to reach the larger Refuge de Clarans, although the nature of the terrain and the difficulties in navigation would make this a fairly long, hard day for most walkers. The day from Clarans to Prat-Redon is quite a long one, but it could be cut short by staying the night at the Cabane de Rieutort, although this is some way off (and below!) the route of the GR 10. The final day from Prat-Redon to Mérens-les-Vals is little more than a half-day's walk.

From the auberge at Siguer follow the GR 10 sign pointing up the hillside from the main street of the village. This is an obvious, wide, albeit steep path. Pass the last telephone box before Mérens-les-Vals and walk to the top end of Gestiès village to find an enclosed footpath. This ascends gradually to emerge onto open hillside and leads to the Col de Gamel (4565ft;1390m). Navigation can be a little tricky in this area. Turn south-south-west for a little while before picking up waymarks leading in a south-easterly direction along the Crête de la Bède to the Pla de Montchamp (6253ft;1904m). Descend towards the south to the Col du Sasc (5905ft;1798m) and observe the dirt road to your left (there is a small cabane near to here where there may be shelter). Maintain direction, eventually crossing the dirt track and reaching the Refuge de Courtal Marti. The cabane is private and locked, but there is water available here. (One report suggested that it might be possible to overnight here, with the permission of the resident shepherds.) Descend steeply to the Refuge de Balledreyt (5255ft;1600m). This is not an ideal overnight stop as the cabane is quite small, suitable for only about three people. There is water available from the nearby stream and the site is not an unattractive one, and certainly is "far from the madding crowd."

It has been reported in recent years that the Refuge de Balledreyt is now in a very sorry state of repair (holes in the roof, very small sleeping platform, etc) making it very uncomfortable or even unsuitable for habitation. The use of a tent in this region is strongly advised.

SECTION 5: DAY 11

REFUGE DE BALLEDREYT to REFUGE DE CLARANS

DISTANCE:	4.7 miles	(7.6km)
ASCENT:	1225ft	(373m)
DESCENT:	2966ft	(903m)

	Timings Sect.	Accum.	Shop	Bar/ Café	Restau- rant	Accomm- odation
REFUGE DE BALLEDREYT			-	-	-	C
JASSE DE SIRBAL	.30	.30	-	-	-	-
COL DE SIRMONT	.50	1.20	-	-	-	-
COUDENES	2.10	3.30	-	-	-	-
REFUGE DE CLARANS	.10	3.40	-	-	-	C

From the Refuge de Balledreyt head south for a little while to reach the mountain stream and then follow this down in an east-north-easterly direction to a clearing at the Jasse de Sirbal (4434ft;1350m). The old route of the GR 10 continues in the same direction along the Sirbal to reach a road above the Grange de Sigueille. Turn left here for the numerous facilities of Aston and Les Cabannes (quite a lengthy detour) or right up the road to reach Coudènes. The new route of the GR 10, however, crosses the river at the Jasse de Sirbal and ascends steeply through woodland to arrive at an open plateau. This is the wide Col de Sirmont (5560ft;1693m) between the summits of Sirmont to the north-east and Massayre to the south-east.

The descent from the Col de Sirmont can be rather confusing and difficult to negotiate. It is essential that the correct line of descent is taken as the area is surrounded by steep and precipitous hillside. Aim in a south-south-westerly direction to pick up red / white waymarks and descend very steeply to the river. Despite considerable improvements in the waymarking generally in the Ariège, the descent from the Col de Sirmont still requires care. The route, at least initially, seems to be a little to the east of the line shown on the IGN map, but the waymarking steadily improves with a loss of altitude. Continue the descent, now on a reasonable footpath and passing mainly through woodland, to reach a footbridge near to the road at Coudènes (3416ft;1040m). Walk over the footbridge, cross the road and take a waymarked path opposite. After a while bear away from the main route towards the north for a short distance to reach the Refuge de Clarans (3514ft;1070m). This cabane can accommodate about five people and has a fireplace and a water supply. It has been reported that the Refuge de Clarens is now dirty and uninviting, so that those carrying a tent will once again have a great advantage.

Note that the old route of the GR 10 left Coudènes and took a trail via Laparan, the Cabane de Rieutort, Etang de Ruille and the Col de Terre Nègre to rejoin the new route of the GR 10 (described here) at the Col de Belh.

SECTION 5: DAY 12

REFUGE DE CLARANS to REFUGE DE PRAT-REDON

DISTANCE:	11 miles	(17.7km)
ASCENT:	4296ft	(1308m)
DESCENT:	1869ft	(569m)

	Timings Sect.	Accum.	Shop	Bar/ Café	Restau- rant	Accomm- odation
REFUGE DE CLARANS			-	-	-	C
CABANE D'ARTARAN	2.00	2.00	-	-	-	C?
REFUGE DE BEILLE D'EN HAUT	1.30	3.30	-	-	-	-
COL DE LA DIDORTE	2.50	6.20	-	-	-	-
COL DE BELH	1.45	8.05	-	-	-	-
REFUGE DE PRAT-REDON	1.00	9.05	-	-	-	C

Quite a long stage in fairly remote countryside. The highlight of the walk is the impressive Crête des Isards which offers wide views over to the peaks forming the Franco-Spanish border. An alternative overnight can now be made in the new, guarded Refuge du Ruhle

At the Jasse d'Artaran

(over 50 places). The route of the GR 10 in this region now links with this new hut and is different from that described in this book below (followthe recent IGN map and the current waymarking).

From the Refuge de Clarans rejoin the GR 10 and climb steeply through woodland. The route is well waymarked and leads to a high level plateau and the Cabane d'Artanan (5567ft;1695m). This is used by shepherds and herdsmen but it may be possible to stay the night there. From the cabane head north-north-east to reach a dirt road where you turn right. Note that where this unmade road is joined ("Cabane des Isarges" on the IGN map) there is now a cross-country skiing centre likely to be closed during the summer months, but the café / restaurant may be open. There are several cabanes marked on the map in this area, but they are probably private and / or unsuitable for an overnight stop. Follow the unmade road to reach the Refuge de Beille d'en Haut. This is private and is used to store animals.

From this hut head in a south-easterly direction on a fairly obvious path along a ridge passing Prat Moll (6565ft;1999m) and a second top at 6512ft (1983m) before descending past a ruined cabane to the Col des Finestres. The GR 10 continues in the same direction keeping to the ridge to reach the Col de la Didorte (6874ft;2093m). If an overnight stop is now required then a steep descent down the grassy hillside

View from the Crête des Isards

leads in about 30 minutes to the Cabane de Rieutort at 5977ft (1820m). This is a pleasant cabane suitable for up to six people and was on the old route of the GR 10. There is a fireplace and the stream outside is rich in trout (it is a popular place for anglers; the walker may be lucky and get treated to a free fish supper!) The disadvantage of this hut is that it involves a descent of 897ft (273m) from the route of the GR 10, which of course must be regained the following morning. It has been reported that if accommodation is sought in this area, a better alternative to the Cabane de Rieutort is a new cabane at Etang d'Embizon. It is on the opposite side of the ridge and closer to the GR 10 in both distance and altitude.

From the Col de la Didorte keep to the ridge heading south-east to reach a height of 7481ft (2278m). From here, above the Etang d'Embizon, the circular Tour des Montagnes d'Ax begins, heading north-north-east to Le Castelet and Ax-les-Thermes. However the GR 10 keeps to the ridge heading south, then bears south-west to traverse the Crête des Isards. There are steep drops on either side of the ridge but little difficulty should be experienced. There are fine views all around. The crest undulates until the Col de Belh (or Beil) at 7379ft (2247m). Here take a change in direction to descend east-north-east down the ravine, following the course of the river until a wide, level area is reached in which is situated the Refuge de Prat-Redon. This is a pleasant spot by the river. The cabane has space for up to eight people. There is a table and chair and a fireplace. This cabane has recently been thoroughly and comfortably renovated (work of the Syndicat d'Initiative of Ax-les-Thermes). There is also a similarly renovated cabane further on at the Jasse des Llerbes (see next section).

SECTION 5: DAY 13

REFUGE DE PRAT-REDON to MERENS-LES-VALS

DISTANCE:	9.6 miles	(15.5km)
ASCENT:	1793ft	(546m)
DESCENT:	4256ft	(1296m)

	Timings					
	Sect.	Accum.	Shop	Bar/ Café	Restau- rant	Accomm- odation
REFUGE DE PRAT-REDON			-	-	-	C
COUILLADE DE LLERBES	2.20	2.20	-	-	-	-
COL DU SAVIS	1.00	3.20	-	-	-	-
PONT DE PIERRES	1.20	4.40	-	-	-	-
MERENS-LES-VALS	.50	5.30	++	++	++	G. H

This last section to Mérens-les-Vals should offer no great difficulties. After an initial climb the rest is more or less downhill. If an early start is made, Mérens-les-Vals should be reached by lunchtime which allows plenty of time for relaxing, re-stocking with provisions and enjoying a good meal.

Leave the refuge, cross the stream and ascend steeply towards the east-south-east. At the top of the ridge continue for a while in the same direction before turning north on a fairly good path. Reach the Couillade de Llerbès, an area much eroded owing to numerous ski developments. Turn towards the south, following a track for a while to pass under a ski-lift. The waymarking is generally quite good along this section. Cross the river (Ruisseau des Estagnols) and turn to the north-east. After the Col de Savis (6253ft;1904m) the GR 10 turns again, this time to the south-south-west. After finally reaching woodland the trail makes a sharp turn to the north-east. Mérens-les-Vals comes into view in the Ariège valley below. Descend on a well defined path following the course of the river. Cross an old bridge (the Pont des Pierres) and continue down through the trees to emerge eventually in the high street of Mérens-les-Vals (3481ft;1060m).

For the gîte d'étape (recommended) cross the main street and ascend past the crucifix, following the red/white markings to a road. Here turn left and descend for about 300 yards to the gîte. This gîte d'étape (which doubles as a youth hostel) serves excellent meals; the evening meal in particular is high in both quality and quantity.

Mérens-les-Vals although quite small has a food shop (limited range of provisions) and and also a railway station. The train goes down the Ariège valley to Ax-les-Thermes, a large centre with numerous shops, supermarkets, hotels and banks (note that there is no bank in Mérens-les-Vals).

INTRODUCTION

From Mérens-les-Vals the GR 10 leaves the Ariège behind and enters the Eastern Pyrenees, the Pyrénées Orientales. The first few days are in most spectacular scenery, passing close to the jagged granite massif of Pic Carlitte and overcoming the steep and often snow-covered passes of the Porteille des Bésines, the Col de Coume d'Agnel and the Porteille de la Grave. The route travels eastwards, crossing the high-level plateau of Cerdagne to reach the picturesque villages of Mantet and Py. From here the GR 10 traverses the Canigou massif before descending to the Vallespir valley at Arles-sur-Tech. The last few days from here to the coast are in typical Mediterranean country which can be both dry and hot during the summer months. The Pyrénées Orientales has much grandeur, variety of scenery and, unlike much of the isolated Ariège, it includes several popular holiday areas.

The Pic Carlitte region is justifiably popular with mountain walkers. The area has many fine mountain lakes, streams and rocky peaks. The GR 10 does not include the summit of Pic Carlitte (9593ft;2921m) but if time and energy are available it is a recommended detour from the main route.

Cerdagne and Roussillon are the Catalan speaking areas of France. Unlike the language of the Basques, Catalan is an Indo-European language, something of a cross between French and Spanish. The Catalan provinces span the border between France and Spain and indeed the French Catalans often sound and seem to be more Spanish than French. The Catalonians, like the Basques, have long campaigned for autonomy. There is a strong regional pride and identity; the visitor will notice many red and yellow Catalan flags in the larger towns.

The Cerdagne is entered on the GR 10 at the Col de la Perche. This region comes as quite a surprise. It is basically a wide and extensive plateau at an altitude of around 5000ft (1522m). There are several small towns and villages in the area, the principal of which is the fortified town of Mont Louis. The GR 10 gets to within a mile or so of here before visiting the village of Planès with its unusual shaped church.

The Cerdagne is served by a narrow gauge tourist train. The 'little yellow train' runs from Villefranche-de-Confluent down in the Têt valley up to Mont Louis and on to Bourg-Madame and Latour-de-Carol. It may be of use to the GR 10 wayfarer who wishes to terminate or pick-up the route in this area. Alternatively a ride on this train on a rest day would be a very pleasant way of exploring the Têt and Carol valleys.

The Pic du Canigou is the most prominent and revered mountain in the Eastern Pyrenees. While this impressive peak is officially excluded from the route of the GR 10, most people will wish to claim the summit. The ascent provides no great difficulty in good weather conditions. It is really the last great barrier before the Mediterranean and the view from this lofty perch is very extensive.

The Tech (or Vallespir) valley is met at historic Arles-sur-Tech where there is a 9th century abbey church tucked away amongst the numerous side-streets. The neighbouring region has a hot and dry climate during the summer months, the amount of annual rainfall being very significantly lower than in the Western Pyrennes. Upstream from Arles are the Gorges de la Fou, said to be the narrowest gorges in the world and a visit would provide another worthwhile day-off.

The profile of the eastern end of the Pyrenean chain is very different from that in the west where the foothills and mountains gradually gain in height with distance from the Atlantic. In the east the land remains relatively high until just before the coast where the mountains and the GR 10 finally descend to reach the Mediterranean sea.

The GR 10 ends at Banyuls-sur-Mer on the Côte Vermeille. This stretch of coastline runs from Argèles-sur-Mer to the border with Spain at Cerbère. Banyuls-sur-Mer itself is not particularly inspiring, although the tired walker will more than likely wish to spend an hour or so soaking up the sun on the small but popular beach. Collioure, a 15-minute train journey from Banyuls-sur-Mer, is much more interesting and well worth a visit. It was once a thriving fishing community, but now its harbour, church and lighthouse are much visited by tourists and its cafés and beauty spots often frequented by artists.

A visit to Perpignan is highly recommended before returning home. The capital of Catalonia has an impressive gothic cathedral and the Palace of the Kings of Mallorca. The tower of this building provides a good viewpoint from where one can look out over the roofs of Perpignan and over the plain of Roussillon to the south for a final view of the mountains of the Pyrenees.

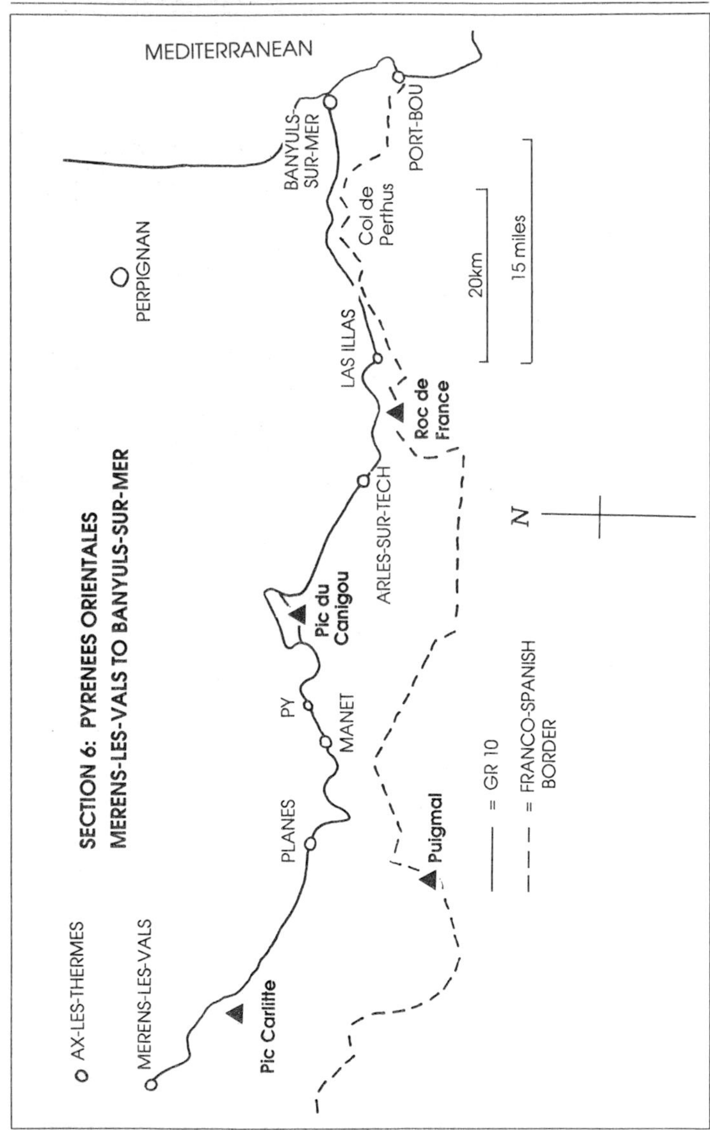
SECTION 6: PYRENEES ORIENTALES
MERENS-LES-VALS TO BANYULS-SUR-MER
MEDITERRANEAN
AX-LES-THERMES
MERENS-LES-VALS
Pic Carlitte
PLANES
Puigmal
PY
MANET
Pic du Canigou
ARLES-SUR-TECH
Roc de France
LAS ILLAS
PERPIGNAN
Col de Perthus
BANYULS-SUR-MER
PORT-BOU
20km
15 miles
N
= GR 10
= FRANCO-SPANISH BORDER

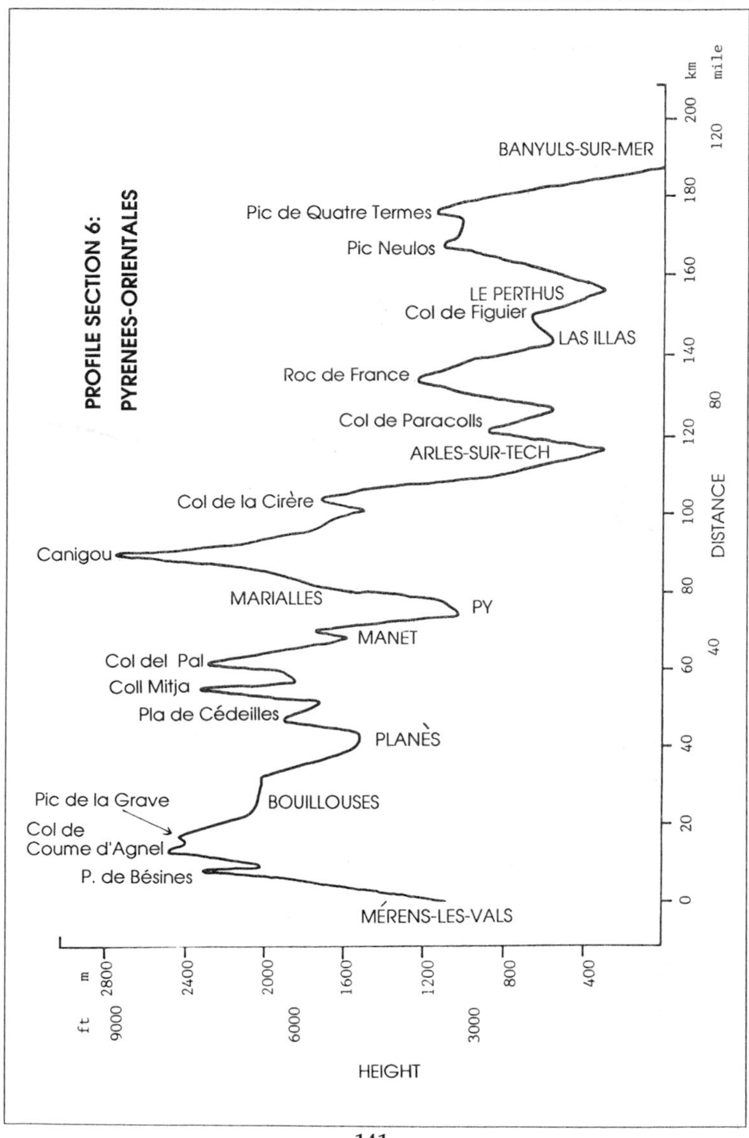
PROFILE SECTION 6:
PYRENEES-ORIENTALES
BANYULS-SUR-MER
Pic de Quatre Termes
Pic Neulos
LE PERTHUS
Col de Figuier
LAS ILLAS
Roc de France
Col de Paracolls
ARLES-SUR-TECH
Col de la Cirère
Canigou
MARIALLES
PY
MANET
Col del Pal
Coll Mitja
Pla de Cédeilles
PLANÈS
BOUILLOUSES
Pic de la Grave
Col de
Coume d'Agnel
P. de Bésines
MÉRENS-LES-VALS
km
mile
0
20
40
60
80
100
120
140
160
180
200
40
80
120
DISTANCE
m
2800
2400
2000
1600
1200
800
400
ft
9000
6000
3000
HEIGHT

SECTION 6: DAY 1

MERENS-LES-VALS to REFUGE DES BESINES

DISTANCE:	$5^{1/2}$ miles	(8.9km)
ASCENT:	4181ft	(1273m)
DESCENT:	1156ft	(352m)

	Timings					
	Sect.	Accum.	Shop	Bar/ Café	Restau- rant	Accomm- odation
MERENS-LES-VALS			++	++	++	G H
JASSE DE PRESSASSE	2.30	2.30	-	-	-	-
PORTEILLE DES BESINES	1.30	4.00	-	-	-	-
REFUGE DES BESINES	.50	4.50	-	-	-	C

This is a rather short day but in magnificent surroundings. On the ascent to the Porteille des Bésines keep an eye out for isard as they tend to be numerous in this area.

It would be possible for a strong party to reach the CAF refuge at the Barrage des Bouillouses (see Section 6, Day 2), but this would make for a very long, hard day. The backpacker will enjoy camping in this majestic area.

The GR 10 is once again entering an area of high mountains and for the next few days, until east of the Pic du Canigou, the route is often above the 2000m mark.

From the centre of Mérens-les-Vals follow the description to the gîte d'étape (Section 5, Day 13). From the gîte ascend on a good path heading to the south-east, soon passing an ancient church. The route is well waymarked and should never be in doubt as it climbs steadily to a plateau at 6017ft (1832m). This is the Jasse de Préssassé and from here the route turns to head in a southerly direction, climbing more steeply to reach the Porteille des Bésines (7662ft;2333m) which is dominated by a large cairn.

Maintain direction to descend steeply at first and then more gently until the small cabane (Refuge des Bésines) is reached. This is situated at a height of 6506ft (1981m). There is space for about five people and water is in plentiful supply. If this cabane is full then there is another one about half a mile away to the west, at the other end of the small lake. This is the Refuge du Barrage des Bésines (marked on the 1:50,000 IGN map). This offers accommodation for about six people.

SECTION 6: DAY 2

REFUGE DES BESINES to BARRAGE DES BOUILLOUSES

DISTANCE:	$10^{1/2}$ miles	(16.9km)
ASCENT:	2677ft	(815m)
DESCENT:	2549ft	(776m)

	Timings					
	Sect.	Accum.	Shop	Bar/ Café	Restau- rant	Accomm- odation
REFUGE DES BESINES			-	-	-	C
COL DE COUME D'AGNEL	1.45	1.45	-	-	-	-
PORTEILLE DE LA GRAVE	1.30	3.15	-	-	-	-
BARRAGE DES BOUILLOUSES	2.30	5.45	-	+	+	R

The first part of today's journey passes through grand, wild country. On the ascent to the Col de Coume d'Agnel snowfields will almost certainly be encountered, but these should present no great difficulty.

In the vicinity of the Etang de Lanoux the GR 10 crosses the GR 7, another long distance route on its way north from Andorra. Once over the Porteille de la Grave the wilderness disappears and scores of tourists are often met enjoying the fishing, fresh air and scenery of the Vallée de la Grave. The whole of today's route is generally well waymarked and much of it is on clear, well used paths.

A recommended alternative to today's official route is to leave the GR 10 at the small hut below the Col de Coume d'Agnel and take the GR 7 above the south-east shore of the Etang de Lanoux until in the vicinity of the Refuge de la Guimbarde. From here there is a route to the summit of Pic Carlitte (9593ft;2921m). This is the line of the HRP. It can be followed to the Barrage des Bouillouses. Pic Carlitte is the highest summit in the Eastern Pyrenees and offers a fine panorama.

From the Refuge des Bésines cross the stream and ascend in an east-north-easterly direction. After a while the route steepens considerably and several snowfields will have to be negotiated before the top of the pass is reached at 8112ft (2470m). Some walkers have reported the area to be snowless in mid-August. Do not descend directly down the snowfield on the Col de Coume d'Agnel (this is steep and potentially dangerous), instead avoid the snow by keeping to the left a little then head south-east for the edge of the Etang de Lanoux. Ascend slightly to reach a level area where there is a small cabane and where the GR 7 from Andorra meets the GR 10. The obvious col ahead is the Porteille de la Grave (7967ft;2426m) which is climbed on a good path.

From the col descend steeply at first to pick up a very clear path heading in a south-easterly direction down the Vallée de la Grave with the river over to the left. On reaching the Lac des Bouillouses turn to the south to follow an undulating, rock strewn path along the western shore of the lake. Cross the Barrage des Bouillouses to reach the CAF hut. This refuge has road access and is more in the nature of an hotel than a mountain hut. There are several small dormitories and a café and restaurant. There is a kitchen area where one's food can be prepared. The showers are expensive but worth every franc!

There is also a hotel on the west side of the dam. The café / restaurant on the east side of the barrage also runs a refuge, reported to be rather scruffy but cheaper than the CAF refuge down the road.

SECTION 6: DAY 3

BARRAGE DES BOUILLOUSES to REFUGE DE L'ORRY

DISTANCE:	14½ miles	(23.3km)
ASCENT:	1980ft	(603m)
DESCENT:	2670ft	(813m)

	Timings Sect.	Accum.	Shop	Bar/ Café	Restau-rant	Accomm-odation
BARRAGE DES BOUILLOUSES			-	+	+	R
COL DEL PAM	1.30	1.30	-	-	-	-
PYRENEES 2000	.15	1.45	++	++	++	H+
BOLQUERE	.25	2.10	+	+	+	H+
COL DE LA PERCHE	.40	2.50	-	-	-	-
LA CABANASSE	.45	3.35	++	+	+	(G) (CP)
PLANES	.50	4.25	-	-	-	(G) (CP)
PLA DE CEDEILLES	1.10	5.35	-	-	-	-
REFUGE DE L'ORRY	1.05	6.40	-	-	-	C

This section is very different from the wild grandeur of the preceding 2 days. There are wooded hillsides and the high-level plain of Cerdagne in which several villages and small towns are scattered. Unfortunately, because of the convenient road and rail connections there are now several tourist centres and skiing facilities. The most garish of these is the Pyrénées 2000 village. This is not actually on the route of the GR 10 but it is all too easy to lose the line of the path in the vicinity of Pyrénées 2000 and end up wandering past its hotels and shopping centres. The walking is generally of an easy nature with relatively little ascent or descent. The famous 'little yellow train' runs through this high plateau land and the nearest station is situated at La Cabanasse. There are several opportunities to buy food, but remember to make a final replenishment of supplies at La Cabanasse as the next épicerie is at Mantet. On leaving Planès the scenery improves and one can then look forward to several further days in impressive surroundings.

From the CAF refuge turn left and walk down the road for about 500 yards. Cross the small bridge over the river on the right and walk south-west for a short way before turning south, keeping the wood to the left. It can become a little confusing in this region but a small refuge should soon be reached on the left. From here make for the track ahead keeping the lake on the left. This track shortly enters a wood. After a while leave the main track (which descends at this point) and take a path off to the right. Continue on this path to the ski-station at the Col de Pam (6585ft;2005m). There are several confusing paths in the area and so alertness is essential. Head south and descend to the road. If the correct path is lost then follow the ski-lift down to the large ski-resort of Pyrénées 2000. There is a small supermarket here and several cafés, restaurants and hotels.

Follow the road downhill to cross the D 118 road. Continue on the road signposted to Bolquère. On reaching the village descend on the Rue de la Perche to the main road (N 116) at the Col de la Perche. Cross the N 116 and take the road opposite. After about 200 yards take the track on the left with wood on right. Follow this to the road at La Cabanasse. Walk down the high street where there is an épicerie and a bread shop. Ignore the sign to Mont Louis (where there is a campsite and a gîte d'étape, La Cassagne) and follow the red and white waymarks to a sign indicating Planès on a lamp-post. The narrow, overgrown footpath emerges at an open field. Turn left along the field edge for 100 yards before turning right onto a second overgrown path. This undulating route continues to the road. Turn left and descend to the village of Planès. Here the GR 36 and the European route E 4 joins the GR 10. The three routes are coincident until the GR 10 parts company with the other two paths east of the Pic du Canigou.

Pass the telephone box and turn right up the road to the old church (worth a visit). Take the path immediately to the left of the church and follow the sign to Pla de Cédeilles. Climb the wide track keeping left at any track division (note that there are several black/white marks and numbers on trees along this track, but few red/white flashes).

Arriving at the Pla de Cédeilles (6276ft;1911m) bear right and follow an undulating narrow path until the river is approached on the left. The cabane will be seen on the opposite bank. Continue well past the hut to reach and cross the bridge across the river. Return to the Refuge de l'Orry. The cabane has room for up to twelve people but is often crowded. However, there are several good flat areas on which to pitch a tent.

SECTION 6: DAY 4

REFUGE DE L'ORRY to MANTET

DISTANCE:	12 miles	(19.2km)
ASCENT:	3862ft	(1176m)
DESCENT:	4716ft	(1436m)

	Timings Sect.	Accum.	Shop	Bar/ Café	Restau- rant	Accomm- odation
REFUGE DE L'ORRY			-	-	-	C
COLL MITJA	2.20	2.20	-	-	-	-
REFUGE DU RAS DE LA CARANCA	.50	3.10	-	-	-	R
JASSE DES CLOTS	1.10	4.20	-	-	-	-
COLL DEL PAL	1.15	5.35	-	-	-	-
MANTET	2.00	7.35	+	+	+	G (2)

Both woodland and high mountain passes are encountered on this section with views over to the Canigou massif. Mantet is an old Pyrenean village of great character. Its popularity with walkers is reflected in the fact that there are two gîtes d'étape in the village.

From the Refuge de l'Orry descend with the river on the left, passing an old wooden cabane on the right before finally bearing right to an intact cabane. Leave the track here and strike out to the right, following the red and white waymarks to climb steeply. Emerge at a track where you turn right. This track climbs to the summit of the pass, but leave and rejoin it several times to climb more steeply following the red/ white flashes. Eventually Coll Mitja is attained at 7774ft (2367m). The route can be a little difficult to follow in the lower reaches of the ascent to Coll Mitja. If in doubt follow the track downhill from the Refuge de l'Orry and turn right immediately before a small reservoir. Climb to reach a track which is followed around a large hairpin bend (still climbing) to pick up eventually a path with occasional waymarks for the final ascent to Coll Mitja

From the summit of the col bear over to the left to pick up a wide track. Follow this downhill through numerous zig-zags to reach the Refuge de la Caranca (room for about fourteen people; warden during the main season, food and drink available to non-residents).

Continue past this refuge with the river on the left for about 100 yards before crossing this river by a small bridge. Follow a path through woodland to reach a small ruined stone hut on the right at the Jasse des Clots. From here strike out across scrub to locate a path climbing steeply to the Coll del Pal (7534ft;2294m). Continue to skirt the hillside in a south-easterly direction on a narrow path. After a while begin the steep descent. Soon the village of Mantet is seen way below. Just before the village cross the river by a footbridge and climb up to Mantet. Apart from the two gîtes d'étape, there is also a restaurant in the village and small quantities of supplies may be purchased. In addition Mantet boasts two auberges/restaurants (the one in the middle of the village run by M. Peronne ["El Tupi'] is highly recommended).

SECTION 6: DAY 5

MANTET to MARIAILLES

DISTANCE:	7.8 miles	(12.5km)
ASCENT:	3304ft	(1006m)
DESCENT:	2752ft	(838m)

	Timings Sect.	Accum.	Shop	Bar/ Café	Restau- rant	Accomm- odation
MANTET			+	+	+	G (2)
PY	2.00	2.00	+	+	+	G
COL DE JOU	1.30	3.30	-	-	-	-
MARIAILLES	1.45	5.15	-	-	-	R

Neither a long nor a particularly inspiring day. The oddly named village of Py is an attractive place and it may be worthwhile to spend the heat of the day enjoying a meal at the Bar-Restaurant de la Fontaine. Supplies can also be purchased at this establishment; these will be needed for the next 2 days through the Canigou region. Py also has a gîte d'étape and it may be difficult to abandon this for the simple pleasures of a night at Mariailles. Indeed it is possible to make the Chalet des Cortalets in one day from Py, but this makes for a long, hard march, particularly if the summit of the massif is included in the itinerary.

Leave Mantet heading in a north-easterly direction aiming for the obvious col above the village (the Col de Mantet). Several rough paths are found on this hillside, but if in difficulty follow the line of the telegraph poles (some with red/white flashes on them).

On reaching the Col de Mantet (5783ft;1761m) take a path descending for a few yards to a gate. Pass through this and descend through woodland to the road. Descend into the valley on this road, taking two short cuts from it where indicated by red/white markings. Eventually rejoin the road down to the village of Py at 3360ft (1023m).

Descend through the village to reach the road again. Take the first footpath off to the right (GR 10 sign on wall, easily missed). Follow a narrow path that contours round the mountainside and climbs to emerge eventually at a road at the Col de Jou (3695ft;1125m). Here you enter the region of the Canigou massif. Alternative routes lead from here to Casteil or to Vernet-les-Bains via the Tour de Goa. Food and lodgings may be found at these locations. However, for the GR 10 cross the road at the Col de Jou and follow the track up through the woods (signposted Mariailles 1hr 30mins). Note that yellow arrow markers accompany the red/white flashes from here on. The yellow markers lead eventually to the summit of the Pic du Canigou. Follow the obvious track and paths to the forest clearing at Mariailles (5642ft;1718m) where the Refuge de Mariailles (guarded - 40 places - excellent food) will be found.

SECTION 6: DAY 6

MARIAILLES to CHALET DES CORTALETS

DISTANCE:	Via Pic du Canigou:	6.8 miles	(11km)
	Via Col de Segalès:	8.7 miles	(14km)
ASCENT:	Via Pic du Canigou:	3829ft	(1166m)
	Via Col de Segalès:	3255ft	(991m)
DESCENT:	Via Pic du Canigou:	2411ft	(734m)
	Via Col de Segalès:	1836ft	(559m)

	Timings Sect.	Timings Accum.	Shop	Bar/ Café	Restau- rant	Accomm- odation
MARIAILLES			-	-	-	R
BRANCH POINT OF 2 ROUTES	1.45	1.45	-	-	-	-
REFUGE ARAGO	.20	2.05	-	-	-	C
PIC DU CANIGOU	1.40	3.45	-	-	-	-
CHALET DES CORTALETS	1.45	5.30	-	+	+	R. H
(COL DE SEGALES)	(30)	(2.15)	-	-	-	-
(REFUGE DE BONNE-AIGUE)	(2.00)	(4.15)	-	-	-	C
(CHALET DES CORTALETS)	(1.30)	(5.45)	-	+	+	R. H

(Note that timings for the GR 10 via the Col de Seagalès are given in brackets.)

Today's route through the Canigou massif traverses some of the best scenery in the Eastern Pyrenees. The official route of the GR 10 avoids the summit of Canigou, preferring a detour to the west via the Col de Segalès. However a traverse of the mountain itself is highly recommended and provides a highlight on this stage of the walk, the summit being the highest point reached on the entire crossing from

Part of the Canigou massif

Atlantic to Mediterranean.

The ascent of the mountain from the south should not, however, be underestimated and this route should definitely be avoided in mist or storm conditions, or by walkers unused to scrambling with heavy rucksacks. The summit ridge of the Pic de Canigou is rocky and as the highest point in the vicinity it would be a very dangerous place to be in an electrical storm. The scrambling, albeit strenuous, is fairly easy provided that the yellow markers are followed carefully. These lead sensationally to the summit cairn. It must be stressed that neither the official route nor the summit variant should be attempted in bad weather.

Another alternative for those wishing to "bag" the summit of Canigou would be to arrive early at the Chalet des Cortalets, claim accommodation and then make the ascent from there, returning for an overnight at the hotel or refuge. The majority of the contents of a backpack could then be left at the Chalet des Cortalets for the ascent/ descent of the peak.

The GR 10 leads south from Mariailles (signposted Col de Segalès and Refuge Arago). The path climbs steadily through wooded mountainside heading generally towards the north-east. After crossing the River Cady you climb more steeply for a while before reaching a bifurcation of paths. The official GR 10 continues on to the Col de Segalès, but for the recommended route to the Pic du Canigou turn right here and follow the yellow arrows. The path leads to the Refuge Arago, a small cabane suitable for only two to three people, then climbs to the summit of the Pic du Canigou with yellow waymarks all the way to the top. After a while the path steepens, the ascent becoming increasingly harder until the last 150 feet when both hands and feet must be used to negotiate large rocks and boulders. The route emerges suddenly at the summit where there is a large cross together with a panoramic table. The peak at 9143ft (2784m) is the highest point in Catalonia and affords an extensive view.

Descend from the mountain on the obvious tourist route, heading in a northerly direction. Eventually bear right to pick up the red and white markers and so rejoin the official GR 10 route. This leads to the Chalet des Cortalets at 7061ft (2150m). The hotel and restaurant are very popular with tourists, there being a motorable road to this point. There is a CAF refuge adjacent to the Chalet. This is really more like a cabane as there is no guardian and the inside is somewhat dirty and primitive, with few facilities other than bunk-beds upstairs and a table downstairs. Payment for the night is made at the Chalet des Cortalets.

GR 10 via Col de Segalès

This route is well waymarked throughout with the usual red/white flashes. Continue from the branchpoint of the two routes to walk on a level path heading at first towards the north-west. On reaching the Col de Segalès (6700ft;2040m) descend to the north-east on a good path through woodland. Eventually zig-zags lead down to a small cabane (the Refuge de Bonne-Aigue at 5718ft;1741m). From here climb a zig-zagging path heading in a south-easterly direction. Pass to the north of Pic Joffre and after a while the tourist route down from the summit of the Pic du Canigou will be met on the right. Continue to follow the waymarks to the Chalet des Cortalets.

SECTION 6: DAY 7

CHALET DES CORTALETS to ARLES-SUR-TECH

DISTANCE:	15½miles	(25km)
ASCENT:	828ft	(252m)
DESCENT:	6962ft	(2120m)

	Timings Sect.	Accum.	Shop	Bar/ Café	Restau- rant	Accomm- odation
CHALET DES CORTALETS			-	+	+	R. H.-
RAS DEL PRAT CABRERA	.50	.50	-	-	-	-
ABRI DU PINATELL	.55	1.45	-	-	-	C
MAISON FORESTIERE DE L'ESTANYOL	.25	2.10	-	-	-	C
COL DE LA CIRERE	.45	2.55	-	-	-	-
MINES DE FER DE BATERE	.30	3.25	-	-	-	-
ARLES-SUR-TECH	3.20	6.45	++	++	++	H+. CP

This is quite a long stage involving about 7000 feet of descent. However there is only one climb involved (up to the Col de la Cirère) and this is relatively short, so most walkers should not find the trek too demanding. This section is a significant one in that the high mountains of the Pyrenees are now being left behind and you are descending to an altitude of only 926ft (282m) at Arles-sur-Tech. This is the first time that the trail has been below the 1000 feet mark since the Basque country in the west. The climate and vegetation change markedly from here on as the Mediterranean region begins to exert its influence.

From the Chalet des Cortalets head north following red/white waymarks through shrub and trees to emerge on a track. Follow this, at first heading in a southerly direction, all the way to Ras del Prat Cabrera (5711ft;1739m). This route is still co-incident with the GR 36 and the E 4. There are plans to provide an alternative route for the GR 10 to the south of that described above.

Leave the track at Ras del Prat Cabrera and head in a southerly direction, descending and traversing the mountainside. The obvious albeit narrow path eventually, after crossing two streams, heads in an easterly direction to reach the Abri du Pinatell (5419ft;1650m). This small, very basic shelter would provide accommodation for about eight people if required. The path continues through woodland to emerge in a clearing at the Maison Forestière de l'Estanyol (or Estagnole) at 4857ft (1479m), a good clean cabane which sleeps sixteen people (water fountain adjacent).From here the Col de la Cirère must first be attained before commencing the long descent to Arles-sur-Tech. Hence take the clear waymarked path, climbing at first towards the south, and follow the Balcon du Canigou to reach the col. The exact height of the Col de la Cirère seems to be in some doubt; it is marked as 1731m (5685ft) on the IGN1:50,000 map, but a notice board on the col itself clearly displays a height of 1806m (5931ft).

Up to this point all the paths and tracks have been clear and well waymarked, but one is now leaving the main Canigou area so perhaps a little more care in navigation may be required. Descend to some ruined mine workings (Mines de Fer de Batère) and from here pick up a track. Follow this as it descends through a series of zig-zags. After passing a gîte-restaurant (good food reported) reach a bend in the road where a path descending to the east should be found. Take this and follow it as it turns to head in a south-easterly direction. Keep to this for some way, but before it starts ascending too much, take another track heading off to the right. Follow this and further paths all heading down towards the south-east, passing some old mine-lift machinery. The route eventually emerges at a road which zig-zags down to the town of Arles-sur-Tech (926ft;282m). There are several hotels to be found here and an abundance of shops, restaurants and cafés. There is a bank and post-office. The campsite is at the western end of the town near the swimming pool (piscine).

SECTION 6: DAY 8

ARLES-SUR-TECH to LAS ILLAS

DISTANCE:	16.2 miles	(26.1km)
ASCENT:	4325ft	(1317m)
DESCENT:	3445ft	(1049m)

	Timings Sect.	Accum.	Shop	Bar/ Café	Restau-rant	Accomm-odation
ARLES-SUR-TECH			++	++	++	H+ CP
COL DE PARACOLLS	1.45	1.45	-	-	-	-
MONTALBA D'AMELIE	1.30	3.15	-	-	-	-
COLL DEL RIC	1.30	4.45	-	-	-	-
ROC DE FRANCE	1.15	6.00	-	-	-	-
LAS ILLAS	2.30	8.30	-	-	+	G. H

Another long day with little opportunity for obtaining accommodation or supplies between Arles-sur-Tech and Las Illas. Furthermore the terrain is now Mediterranean in character and during most of the summer months it is hot and dry with few water sources. Several houses are passed on route where it may be possible to obtain water, although it is better to ensure from the outset that sufficient water to last the day is carried. The last 3 days on the GR 10 are quite different from any that have been experienced before and so provide additional interest and variety. The trail only once goes above the 4000ft (1218m) mark, but there is still plenty of climbing before the sea is reached at Banyuls.

Cross the River Tech by a bridge near to the iron workings and follow the red/white waymarks of the GR 10. There are several changes of direction in the initial stages, so take extra care to look for the double red/white marks which indicate these changes. After a while the path climbs steeply before the angle eases somewhat to reach the Col de Paracolls (2962ft;902m).

From this col descend to a cluster of ruined buildings where the route bears to the right (south) following a path down to a river. Cross this and turn left (do not climb). After passing a house the route emerges onto a road where you turn left. After about quarter of a mile leave this road by taking a footpath on the left. Follow this all the way to Montalba d'Amélie. At the building turn right onto the road. Follow this road as it descends to the river and then climbs. After a while the GR 10 leaves the road by taking a path through the trees on the right. The official route meets and crosses this road several times on the ascent, but it can be somewhat difficult to follow this exactly. If in doubt simply follow the road (there is little traffic) which zig-zags many times on its upward journey to reach the building at Can Félix (water tap in garden, but reported by some to be inaccessible to walkers). Here the GR 10 and the HRP join up and remain more or less together until the end of the trail at Banyuls. The route ascends from Can Félix on a path heading in a south-easterly direction to reach the Col del Ric (3156ft;961m).

Continue the ascent in a south-easterly direction on a path which is often steep. Eventually the way turns to the east to skirt below the Roc de Frausa (Roc de France) on a woodland path. (A short detour will lead to the Roc de France at 4663ft (1420m) if desired.) A well waymarked path signposted to Fontfrèda is then followed through woods. Note that about 20-30 minutes after the Col du Puits de la Neige (east of Roc de Frausa) there is a water fountain on the right-hand side of the path. Eventually a junction is reached where the GR 10 branches right on a path signposted to Las Salines and Las Illas. The route to Las Salines soon leaves the GR 10 (the former route is waymarked with orange stripes which should be ignored). Follow the red / white waymarkings, sometimes with a little difficulty, as the route passes through shrub and woodland to emerge onto a road (the D 131) at La Selve. Note that the route of the GR 10 was altered somewhat in this area in 1992. Use only the latest IGN map and follow the new waymarking carefully. Turn right here and follow the road for about 2 miles as it descends to Las Illas (1806ft;550m). For the gîte d'étape follow the signpost into the village where the new gîte (opened in 1986) will be found in the old Mairie (town hall) building. About 100 yards or so up the road is a hotel-restaurant. There is no épicerie in the village.

SECTION 6: DAY 9

LAS ILLAS to REFUGE DE LA TAGNAREDE

DISTANCE:	16½ miles	(26.6km)
ASCENT:	3136ft	(955m)
DESCENT:	1511ft	(460m)

	Timings Sect.	Timings Accum.	Shop	Bar/ Café	Restau-rant	Accomm-odation
LAS ILLAS			-	-	+	G. H.
COLL DEL PRIORAT	2.15	2.15	-	-	-	-
COL DU PERTHUS	1.00	3.15	++	++	++	H+
SAINT MARTIN DE L'ALBERE	1.20	4.35	-	-	-	-
TV RELAY STATION (PIC NEULOS)	1.45	6.20	-	-	-	-
REFUGE DE LA TAGNAREDE	.25	6.45	-	-	-	C

This is not a particularly interesting stretch and once again the high temperatures often encountered in summer could prove a problem. An early start is advisable in order to reach the Col du Perthus in time for a long lunchtime siesta. Numerous shops, cafés, restaurants, hotels and a money exchange will be found here. These facilities are available because the Col du Perthus is the principal border crossing point between France and Spain for vehicular traffic on the eastern side of the country. The place is often crowded and noisy, and long queues of heavy holiday traffic build-up along the international motorway connecting the two countries. It is rather an unattractive area, but it will provide shade from the fierce mid-day sun. This is the last place to obtain supplies before the coast.

From the gîte d'étape at Las Illas turn left and walk down the road to the bridge. Take the zig-zagging road up to Super Illas and from here continue to follow the red / white waymarks to the Col du Figuier (2250ft;685m). Here turn left on a red / white waymarked sandy track. Follow this all the way to the Coll del Priorat (1507ft;459m), keeping close to the border with Spain. Soon after this col you take a narrow footpath through shrub leading off the track to the right (beware of snakes) to emerge on a road at a ruined house. Turn right on this road and follow it past an archaeological site on the right. After a sharp turn to the left it climbs gradually before descending to Le Perthus.

Descend through the town to turn left at the main road. Turn right at the next junction to pass under the autoroute and climb on the D 71 road. Remain on this road for about $2^{1}/_{2}$ miles. Just after the road passes under a viaduct you turn right on a red/white waymarked path. (Note the many paths in the woods in this area; only take the path that is clearly marked with red/white flashes.) The correct path leads to a road where you turn left and continue to a T-Junction. Here continue ahead on a marked path to pass through a gate at the hamlet of Saint-Martin-de l'Albère (2072ft;631m).

Turn left on the road here and after 150 yards turn right on a marked path climbing through trees. The route soon emerges onto open hillside above. Higher up the path again enters trees. Eventually emerge on the road where you turn left and continue to the TV relay station at the top of the hill (Pic Neulos or Néoulous, 4125ft;1256m). Just before the gates of the relay station take the red/white marked path on the left. This leads around the station into a small section of woodland and then down steeply to the fountain at Tagnarède. Collect water here (the sign indicates that it is undrinkable; however it is a much used source of water and is certainly safe after boiling or on addition of water purifying tablets). Do not walk down the track ahead, but keep above it to the right to follow the French/Spanish border marked here by a wire fence. Soon the CAF refuge of Tagnarède is reached. This cabane (built in 1977) has approximately twelve sleeping places on a wooden platform (no mattresses). There is a table and bench provided. The hut's fireplace can be fuelled with fallen wood from the surrounding trees.

Note that there is now a gîte d'étape at the Col de l'Ouillat (3074ft;936m) between Saint-Martin-de l'Albère and Pic Neulos. The gîte d'étape (recommended; meals provided) is 20 minutes off-route, but a path to it through the forest is waymarked as well as a route back to the GR 10 at the Roc des Trois Thermes. The location of the gîte is superb, with panoramic views over Canigou. From this gîte d'étape it is 7 hours to Banyuls-sur-Mer.

SECTION 6: DAY 10

REFUGE DE LA TAGNAREDE to BANYULS-SUR-MER

DISTANCE:	11 miles	(17.7km)
ASCENT:	1159ft	(353m)
DESCENT:	4591ft	(1398m)

	Timings Sect.	Accum.	Shop	Bar/ Café	Restau-rant	Accomm-odation
REFUGE DE LA TAGNAREDE			-	-	-	C
COL DE L'ORRY	.40	.40	-	-	-	-
PIC DE QUATRE TERMES	.50	1.30	-	-	-	-
PIC DE SAILFORT	1.10	2.40	-	-	-	-
COL DES GASCONS	1.30	4.10	-	-	-	-
BANYULS-SUR-MER	1.15	5.25	++	++	++	H+ CP

(Banyuls-sur-Mer has a railway station (SNCF) for trains to Perpignan and Paris.)

The final stage to the Mediterranean coast will be an emotional experience for many walkers, particularly those who have travelled the whole length of the Pyrenean chain from Hendaye on the Atlantic coast. The walk itself is not particularly arduous although it can be difficult to follow in the early stages, especially in mist. The route runs along the Franco-Spanish border until Pic de Sailfort where the border turns sharply to the south. The GR 10 continues more or less in an easterly direction to meet the sea at Banyuls-sur-Mer. The views out to the coast are first rate, over the plains of Roussillon to Collioure and Argelès-sur-Mer on the Côte Vermeille, and south to the Spanish Costa Brava. The blue Mediterranean will be a welcome sight, but beware of the inevitable 'culture shock' on entering the small seaside resort of Banyuls. It is very different from the mountains that have now been left behind!

Some walkers found the waymarking confusing and erratic on this last section, so vigilance is recommended. Note that between the Pic de Quatre Termes and the Pic de la Carbassere another GR 10 route goes off to the north (shown as a variant on the IGN map). One reader reported that the waymarking on this route is similarly poor. The two

Banyuls-sur-mer

routes rejoin before the Col des Gascons.

Leave the Refuge de la Tagnarède on a clear path heading south-east through the trees. Unfortunately this path soon becomes indistinct. Follow the ridge keeping to the French side of the border, which is marked in most places by a wire fence. On reaching the Col de l'Orry (3199ft;974m) climb to the east and avoid the tops of the Puig de las Basses and the Raz de la Menthe to reach a forest road at the Col de l'Estaque (3360ft;1023m). Climb to the Pic des Pradets (3859ft;1175m) and along the ridge to the Pic de Quatre Termes. Keep to the French side of the border to pass the Pic de la Carbassere which has a small stone tower. After the Col del Pal make the final climb of the GR 10 to attain the Pic de Sailfort (3222ft;981m). Here there is an extensive view of the Mediterranean coast.

Leave the border here, descending quite steeply at first, heading east in the direction of Banyuls-sur-Mer which is now in view. The prominent tower to the left is the Tour Madeloc. Eventually a road is reached. Take several paths steeply down to cross the road several times. At the Col des Gascons (1268ft;386m) walk down the road for c.60 yards before turning off to the left on a path. Reach the Fontaine des Chasseurs (water) and continue on the road to the Col de LLagastera (841ft;256m). Follow several tracks down towards the sea and Banyuls-sur-Mer, avoiding any that veer off in the direction of Collioure. On reaching the outskirts of Banyuls-sur-Mer the campsite should be visible. Continue to follow the red/white waymarks to descend on a path to a tunnel under the railway line. On reaching the Avenue Puig del Mas turn left and follow it down to the beach.

Banyuls-sur-Mer has an abundance of shops, cafés, restaurants, hotels and banks. From here a train may be taken back to England via Paris, or down to Spain at Port-Bou and on to Barcelona.

TOURS and VARIANTS

There are a number of circular walking tours of between 1-6 days duration which are detours from the standard GR 10 route. Most of these tours are waymarked with the usual red/white markings and are shown on IGN 1:50,000 maps. They have two main uses; either as a complete short holiday in themselves and as a means of exploring a particular area, or as a useful point of entry to (or escape from) the GR 10. The points at which the GR 10 meets the various Tours are mentioned in the relevant text. Always check these routes on the map for possible changes.

List of Tours (from west to east)

TOUR 1. **Tour de le Vallée de Barétous**
From Arette-Pierre-Saint-Martin (Section 2, Day 1). The Tour leads north, deeper into France, to climb to the Col de Suscousse and the Col de Lataillade before descending to Barlanès (gîte d'étape). The route then stays at a relatively low level, visiting Aramits and the gîte d'étape at Micalet before turning south to return to the Arette-Pierre-Saint-Martin via Pic Soulaing and the Col de Labays. Approximate duration: 3 days.

TOUR 2. **Tour de la Vallée d'Aspe**
From the gîte d'étape above Lescun (Section 2, Day 2). Approximate duration: 3-4 days.

TOUR 3. **Tour du Pic du Midi d'Ossau**
From Lac de Bious-Artigues (Section 2, Day 4). Described in text (page 71). Strongly recommended. 1-day excursion.

TOUR 4. **Tour de Vallée d'Ossau**
From Gourette (Section 2, Day 5). Approximate duration: 3-4 days. Tours 2 and 4 could be linked via the Col d'Aran to provide an alternative route to the GR 10 from Lescun to Gourette.

TOUR 5. **Tour de la Vallee d'Aure**
The route leaves the GR 10 before the descent to Vielle-Aure (Section 3, Day 6) and rejoins it at the Couret de Latuhe (Section 3, Day 7). Approximate duration: 1-2 days.

TOUR 6. **Tour du Biros**

The Tour leaves the GR 10 at the Refuge de l'Etang d'Araing (Section 4, Day 4) and travels north to Playras (gîte d'étape). From here it traverses the Col de Blazy, Col de Héréchech, Col de Méda, Col des Morères and the Col de l'Arraing to descend to Balacet and Lascoux. Next it climbs to Coume Sèche and Coume Dul before rejoining the GR 10 near to the Cabane de Besset (Section 5, Day 2). Approximate duration: 5 days.

TOUR 7. **Tour du Massif des Trois Seigneurs**

This Tour is connected to the GR 10 by a route heading north from the Port de Saleix (Section 5, Day 7) to the Port de Lers. From here the route is circular visiting Liers (gîte d'étape), Col de Port, Bourgaille (gîte d'étape), Bédeilhac, La Freyte (gîte d'étape), Lapège and Sentenac before returning to the Port de Lers. Approximate duration: 5 days.

TOUR 8. **Tour des Montagnes d'Ax**

The Tour leaves the GR 10 at spot height 2278m above Etang d'Embizon on the ridge heading towards the Crête des Isards (Section 5, Day 12). From here it heads north to descend to the Ax valley at Le Castelet. It follows the valley to Ax-les-Thermes, then on to Orgeix and Orlu and up to the Etang de Naguille before rejoining the GR 10 at the Col de Coume d'Agnel (Section 6, Day 2). The GR 10 can be used together with this Tour to make a circular route of about 5-6 days duration. The usual starting place is Ax-les-Thermes. A section of this Tour could conveniently be used to join the GR 10 from Ax-les-Thermes where there is a SNCF railway station (main-line to Paris).

TOUR 9. **Tour du Tres Esteles**

From the Col de Mantet (Section 6, Day 5) head north over the Pic de Trois Estelles and descend to Escaro (gîte d'étape) via the Maison Forestière de Founguéré. From Escaro a route can be taken (marked Circuit Train Jaune on the 1:50,000 IGN map) to Villefranche-de-Confluent which is a terminus of the 'little yellow train'. Alternatively the Tour can be continued south to Py where the GR 10 is rejoined. Note that this Tour is not waymarked on the ground.

There are several alternative routes over short sections of the GR 10. Most of these are waymarked and shown on the 1:50,000 maps. The following is a list of the main possibilities. Note that this list of variants is not an exhaustive one. The same is true for the list of Tours given above. New routes are often being devised and waymarked, whilst some others are occasionally deleted. There are, of course, footpaths other than those that form part of the official GR 10 and its variants, and it would be possible to devise an almost limitless number of link routes or alternatives.

List of Variants (from west to east)

VARIANT 1. From Col Bagarguiac to Logibar via Larrau (Section 1, Day 7). This is described on page 59.

VARIANT 2. From Cauterets to Luz-Saint-Sauveur via Gavarnie (Section 3). This major variation is highly recommended in good weather conditions. It takes 3 days to complete, ie 2 days longer than the standard route via the Col de Riou. See pages 85 to 98.

VARIANT 3. The GR 10 C. This leaves the GR 10 just after the Lac de l'Oule (Section 3, Day 6) and goes northwards through an area of scattered lakes and tarns to descend to the Vallée de la Gripp. It is about 9 miles (14.5km) in length.

VARIANT 4. From the Couret de Latuhe to Adervielle (Section 3, Day 7) where there is a gîte d'étape. About 2 miles (3.2km).

VARIANT 5. From Loudenvielle (Section 3, Day 7) to Cabane Ourtiga (Section 4, Day 1) by-passing Germ. About $3^{1}/_{2}$ miles (5.6km).

VARIANT 6. The GR 10 D. From the Pas de la Core to Estours (Section 5, Day 3). This is described on page 115. It is the old route of the GR 10. About $7^{1}/_{2}$ miles (12.1km).

VARIANT 7. From Moulin Lauga to Couflens via the Pic de Fonta (Section 5, Day 4). This is again part of the old GR 10 route through the Ariège. It requires some care in navigation. The route is described on page 117. About 9.6 miles (15.5km).

VARIANT 8. From the Jasse de Fouillet to Aulus-les-Bains via the Etang de Guzet (Section 5, Day 6). See page 122. About $5^{1}/_{2}$ miles (8.9km).

VARIANT 9. The GR 10 A. From the Etang d'Izourt (Section 5, Day 8) to the Refuge du Fourcat (CAF). Fine mountain country but a one-way route, ie it is necessary to reverse the route to rejoin the GR 10. About 5.4 miles (8.7km) both ways and 2621ft (798m) of ascent and descent.

VARIANT 10. The GR 10 B. A by-pass of Goulier (Section 5, Days 8 and 9). About 3.6 miles (5.8km).

VARIANT 11. The ascent and traverse of the Pic du Canigou (Section 6, Day 6). This is marked on the 1:50,000 IGN map as the Tour du Canigou (and HRP). It is about 1.9 miles (3.1km) shorter than the GR 10 which avoids the summit, but it involves 575ft (175m) of additional ascent and descent. Highly recommended in good weather conditions. The route is described on page 149.

LIST OF PRINCIPAL COLS AND PEAKS ON THE GR 10

(from west to east)

COL D'IBARDIN	1041ft,	317m.
COL DES TROIS FONTAINES	1849ft;	563m.
COL DES TROIS CROIX	1675ft;	510m.
COL DE MEHATCHE	2351ft;	716m.
PIC D'IPARLA	3429ft;	1044m.
COL D'HARRIETA	2654ft;	808m.
PIC DE BUZLANZELHAY	3376ft;	1028m.
COL D'AHARZA	2411ft;	734m.
COL D'URDANZIA	2854ft;	869m.
VIERGE D'ORISSON	3613ft;	1100m.
COL D'ERROZATE	3534ft;	1076m.
COL BAGARGUIAC	4358ft;	1327m.
COL D'ANHAOU	4542ft;	1383m.
COL DE LA PIERRE SAINT MARTIN	5780ft;	1760m.
PAS DE L'OSQUE	6312ft;	1922m.
PAS D'AZUNS	6151ft;	1873m.
COL DE BARRANCQ	5258ft;	1601m.
HOURQUETTE DE LARRY	6749ft;	2055m.
COL D'AYOUS	7176ft;	2185m.
COL DE PEYREGET	7554ft;	2300m.
COL DE SUZON	6895ft;	2127m.
HOURQUETTE D'ARRE	8095ft;	2465m.
COL DE TORTES	5908ft;	1799m.
COL DE SAUCEDE	5008ft;	1525m.
COL DES BORDERES	3777ft;	1150m.
COL D'ILHEOU	7367ft;	2242m.
COL DE RIOU	6401ft;	1949m.
HOURQUETTE D'OSSOUE	8979ft;	2734m.
COL DE MADAMETE	8240ft;	2509m.
COL D'ESTOUDOU	7422ft;	2260m.
COL DE PORTET	7274ft;	2215m.
COURET DE LATUHE	5209ft;	1586m.
PAS DE COURET	6999ft;	2131m.
COL D'ESPINGO	6373ft;	1910m.
HOURQUETTE DES HOUNTS-SECS	7471ft;	2275m.
COL DE LA COUME DE BOURG	7462ft;	2272m.
COL AOU	6874ft;	2093m.
PAS DE BOUC	7127ft;	2170m.
COL D'AUERAN	7146ft;	2176m.
SERRE D'ARAING	7294ft;	2221m.
COL DE L'ARECH	5918ft;	1802m.
CLOT DU LAC	5980ft;	1821m.
COL DE LA LAZIES	6043ft;	1840m.
COL D'AUEDOLE	5682ft;	1730m.
PAS DE LA CORE	4581ft;	1395m.
COL DU SOULARIL	5186ft;	1579m.
PIC DE FONTA	6348ft;	1933m.
COL DE LA PAUSE	5015ft;	1527m.
COL DE LA SERRE DU CLOT	5077ft;	1546m.
PIC AND COL DE FITTE	4555ft;	1387m.
COL D'ESCOTS	5314ft;	1618m
PORT DE SALEIX	5892ft;	1794m.
COL DE BASSIES	6348ft;	1933m.
COL DE RISOUL	4368ft;	1330m.
COL DE L'ESQUERUS	4818ft;	1467m.
COL DE GRAIL	4877ft;	1485m.
COL DE LERCOUL	5087ft;	1549m.
COL DE GAMEL	4565ft;	1390m.
COL DU SASC	5905ft;	1798m.

COL DE SIRMONT	5560ft;	1693m.
COL DE LA DIDORTE	6874ft;	2093m.
COL DE BELH (BEIL)	7379ft;	2247m.
COUILLADE DE COMBEILLE	7311ft;	2226m.
COUILLADE DE LLERBES	7570ft;	2305m.
COL DU SAVIS	6253ft;	1904m.
PORTEILLE DES BESINES	7662ft;	2333m.
COL DE COUME D'AGNEL	8112ft;	2470m.
PORTEILLE DE LA GRAVE	7967ft;	2426m.
COL DEL PAM	6585ft;	2005m.
COL DE LA PERCHE	5192ft;	1581m.
PLA DE CEDEILLES	6276ft;	1911m.
COLL MITJA	7774ft;	2367m.
COLL DEL PAL	7534ft;	2294m.
COL DE MANTET	5783ft;	1761m.
COL DE JOU	3695ft;	1125m.
COL DE SEGALES	6700ft;	2040m.
PIC DU CANIGOU	9143ft;	2784m.
COL DE LA CIRERE	5685ft;	1731m.
COL DE PARACOLLS	2962ft;	902m.
COLL DEL RIC	3156ft;	961m.
COLL DEL PRIORAT	1507ft;	459m.
COL DU PERTHUS	952ft;	290m.
PIC NEULOS	4125ft;	1256m.
COL DE L'ORRY	3199ft;	974m.
PIC DE QUATRE TERMES	3796ft;	1156m.
PIC DE SAILFORT	3222ft;	981m.
COL DES GASCONS	1268ft;	386m.

* * *

USEFUL FRENCH, PYRENEAN AND BASQUEWORDS

Many of the place names in the Pyrennes are local words not generally used in the French language. Furthermore, in the Basque region Basque names are often used, even on French IGN maps. The nature of the terrain and the presence of man-made features can often be deduced from an understanding of the place name. The glossary of terms given below is certainly not a complete list, but is intended to assist in this task. A few French words likely to be of use to the walker have also been included.

Key: B = Basque word; F = French word; P = Pyrenean term.

Accommodation	HEBERGEMENT (F)
Avalanche	AVALANCHE(F) LIT(P) LITS(P) LIS(P)
Bear	OURS(F) ARTZ(B)
Boundary Stone	MOUGA(B) MUGA(B)
Cabin (Mountain Hut)	CABANE(F) ABRI(F) CORTAL(P) ETCHOLA(B) KAYOLAR(B) CAYOLAR(B)
Cattle Enclosure	ENCLOS A BETAIL(F) CORRAL(P)
Cave	GROTTE(F) COBA(P) COBE(P) FORAT(P) FOURAT(P)
Farm	FERME(F) BORDA(B) BORDE(B)
Footbridge	PASSERELLE(F) ZUBI(B)
Footpath	SENTIER(F)
Forest	FORET(F) BEDE(P) OYHAN(B)
Fronton	This is the wall in a pelota court againstwhich the ball is played. Nearly every Basque village has its fronton, which is often one of the walls of the village church.
Glacier	GLACIER(F) SEILH(P)
Grocer's Shop	EPICERIE(F) ALIMENTATION(F) = foodsupplies RAVITAILLEMENT(F) = re-provisioning of food
Gully	COULOIR(F) CANAU(P) CANAOU(P)
Head of Valley	CLOT(P)
Hollow, Depression	OULE(P) OULETTE(P)
Lake (Mountain Lake or Tarn)	LAC(F) ETANG(F) ESTAN (P) (ESTANY(P) BOUM(P) = small deep lake GOURG(P) or GOURC(P) = deep lake
Limestone Area (Stone)	ARRES(B)
Meadow	PRE(F) PRADERE(P)
Moor (or Heath)	LARRA(B) LARRIA(B)

Mountain	MONTAGNE(F) MENDI(B)
Pass (Mountain Pass or Col or Saddle)	
	COL(F) PORT(P) PORTEILLE(P) PORTILLOUA(B) LEPO(B)
	PAS(P) or PASSE(P) = narrow passage
	HOURQUETTE(P) = steep sided col
	COUILLADE(P) or COLLADE(P) = expansive col.
	ARTHEKA(B) or ARTEKS(B) = passage
Pasture	PATURAGE(F) ARTIGUE(P)
	ESTIBE(P) or ESTIBERE(P) = high-level summer pasture
	JASSE(P) = level pasture
Plateau	PLA(P) PLAN(P) CELHAY(B) ZELHAY(B)
	CALM(P) = high bare plateau
Ravine	RAVIN(F) BARRAC(P)
	BARRANC(P) BARRANCO(P)
Ridge	CRETE(F) ARETE(F) SERRE(P)
	CAP(P) = highest point on a ridge
Rocky Peak or outcrop	PUNTA(P)
Scree	PIERRAILLE(F) CAILLAOUAS(P)
Shepherd's Hut	BERGERIE(F) CUJALA(P) COURTAOA(P) CORTAL(P) OLHA(B)
	ORRIS(P) = stone hut
Shop	MAGASIN(F) VENTA(B) BENTA(B)
Spring (Water Source)	SOURCE(F) FONTAINE(F) FONT(P) FOUNT(P) HONT(P) HOUNT(P) ITHURRI(B) ITHOURRI(B)
Station	GARE(F) = railway station
	GARE-ROUTIERE(F) = bus or coach station
	(CAR(F) = bus or coach)
Stream (Mountain Watercourse)	
	RUISSEAU(F) TORRENT(F) GAVE(P) NESTE(P) ARRIBET(P) RIO(P) RIU(P) RIOU(P) ARRIOU(P) ARRIU(P)ARRIEU(P) ERREKA(B)
Summit	SOMMET(F) GAIN(B) GAGNA(B)
	TUC(P) TUCO(P) = sharp summit
	TURON(P) TUROUN(P) SOUM(P) SOM(P) = rounded summit PUIG (Catalan) = peak
Track (Large Footpath or Way)	
	CHEMIN(F) BIDE(B)
Valley	VAL(F) VALLEE(F) VALLON(F) BAL(P) BAT(P) BATCH(P) VALL(P) ARAN(B)IBAR(B)
	COUME(P) = narrow valley
Water	EAU(F) AGUE(P) AIGUE(P) AYGUE(P) UR(B)
Waterfall	CASCADE(F) PICH(P)
Waymarking	BALISAGE(F)
Wood	BOIS(F) BRACAS(P) CHARA(B) ZUR(B)

LIST OF GITES D'ETAPE AND REFUGES ON OR NEAR THE GR 10

The continuing existence of these facilities should be checked locally. Occasionally new gîtes d'étape and refuges are opened on or near to the Trail (again enquire locally for changes).

(1) Gîte d'étape d'Olhette. Mento Bayta. 15 places. Tel 559.54.00.98
(2) Gîte d'étape du Col des Veaux. Ferme Esteben. 15 places. Meals. Tel 559.29.82.72.
(3) Gîte d'étape de Bidarray. 15 places. Meals. Tel 559.37.71.34.
(4) Gîte d'étape de Saint-Etienne-de-Baïgorry. 30 places. Meals. Tel 559.37.42.39.
(5) Gîte d'étape St.-Jean-Pied-De-Port, 9 Route d'Uhart. Tel 559.37.12.08.
(6) Gîte d'étape d'Iraty. 25 places. Meals. Tel 559.28.51.29.
(7) Gîte d'étape de Logibar. 25 places. Meals. Tel 559.28.61.14.
(8) Gîte d'étape de Sainte-Engrâce. 15 places. Meals. Tel 559.28.61.63.
(9) Maison de la Vallée à la Pierre Saint Martin. 46 places. Meals. Tel 559.34.60.76.
(10) Gîte d'étape d'Issor. At Micalet, to the east of Issor on the Tour de la Vallée de Barétous. 16 places. Tel 559.34.45.01.
(11) Gîte d'étape de Lanne. At Barlanes, 1$^{1}/4$ miles (2km) to the south of Lanne on the Tour de la Vallée de Barétous. 16 places. Tel 559.39.64.31.
(12) Gîte d'étape de Lescun. 20 places. 1 mile (1.6km) west of the village. 20 places. Tel 559.34.71.61.
(13) Gîte d'étape de Lhers. 18 places. Tel 559.34.77.27.
(14) Gîte d'étape de Borce. 18 places. Meals. Tel 559.34.86.40.
(15) Gîte d'étape d'Etsaut. 60 places. Meals. Tel 559.34.88.98.
(16) Refuge de Larry. On the Tour de Vallée d'Aspe. 10 places. No telephone.
(17) Refuge d'Ayous. 30 places. Guardian in summer only. Tel 559.05.37.00.
(18) Refuge du Lac de Bious-Artigues. Open 1/6 to 15/10 and school holidays. Owned by Club Pyrénéa Sports. 45 places. Meals. Tel 559.27.23.11.
(19) Refuge d'Arlet. On the Tour de Vallée d'Aspe. Close to the Spanish border. 36 places. Guardian in summer only. Tel 559.34.87.97.
(20) Gîte d'étape d'Accous. L'Estanguet. On the Tour de Vallée d'Aspe 15 places. Meals. Tel 559.34.72.30.
(21) Gîte d'étape de Cette-Eygun. 30 places. Meals. Tel 559.34.78.83.
(22) Refuge de Labérouat. 40 places. Meals. Open Christmas to September. Tel 559.27.05.83 or 559.34.71.59.
(23) Gîte d'étape d'Osse-en-Aspe. On the Tour de Vallée d'Aspe. 15 places. Tel 559.34.73.23.
(24) Gîte d'étape de Landistou. Close to the route of the Tour de Vallée d'Ossau. 45 places. Meals. Tel 559.71.06.98.

(25) Refuge de Pombie. CAF. On the Tour du Pic du Midi d'Ossau. 48 places and camping. Guardian in summer only. Tel 559.05.31.78.
(26) Chalet de Gabas. 50 places. Tel 559.05.33.14.
(27) Chalet de Gourette. 120 places. Meals. Tel 559.05.10.89.
(28) Gîte d'étape des Eaux Chaudes. On the Tour de Vallée d'Ossau. 14 places. Meals. Tel 559.05.33.52.
(29) Youth Hostel Arrens. 22 places. Meals. Tel 562.97.24.64.
(30) Gîte d'étape d'Arrens-Marsous. 16 places. Meals. Tel 562.97.20.21.
(31) Gîte d'étape des Viellettes. 20 places. Meals. Tel 562.97.14.37.
(32) Refuge d'Ilhéou. Raymond Ritter. 32 places. Guardian in summer only. No telephone.
(33) Gîte d'étape de Cauterets. 20 places. Meals. Tel 562.92.58.07.
(34) Chalet-Refuge du Clot. 15 minutes from the Pont d'Espagne. 45 places. Closed in May and June. Meals. Tel 562.92.54.34.
(35) Refuge des Oulettes de Gaube. CAF. 60 places. Guardian April to October. No telephone.
(36) Refuge de Bayssellance. CAF. 70 places. Guardian in summer only. No telephone.
(37) Chalet de Holle à Gavarnie. CAF. Between Gavarnie and La Station des Espécières. 48 places and camping. Meals. Tel 562.92.48.77.
(38) Gîte d'étape de Luz-Saint-Sauveur. 24 places. Open in summer only. Meals. Tel 562.92.82.15 or 562.92.85.85.
(39) Gîte d'étape de Betouey. 15 places. Tel 562.92.80.83.
(40) Hospitalet de Barèges. 100 places. Open in summer only. Meals. Tel 562.92.68.08.
(41) Chalet-Hôtel d'Orédon. Near the lake, east of the Pic de Néouvielle. 45 places. Open in summer only. Tel 562.36.75.33.
(42) Refuge Campana de Cloutou. CAF. GR 10 C. 25 places. No telephone.
(43) Gîte d'étape de Peyras. 17 places. Tel 562.91.81.41.
(44) Gîte d'étape de Bagnères-de-Bigorre. 32 places. Meals. Tel 562.95.34.68.
(45) Refuge de Bastanet. By the Lacs de Bastan. On GR 10 C. 20 places. Guardian in summer only. Tel 562.98.68.62 or 561.23.07.00.
(46) Refuge du Lac d'Oule. 30 places. Open 15/6 to 30/9. Tel 562.39.40.17 or 562.98.48.62.
(47) Gîte d'étape d'Aulon. On the Tour de la Vallée d'Aure. 15 places. Meals in summer only. Tel 562.39.46.96.
(48) Gîte d'étape d'Azet. On the Tour de la Vallée d'Aure. 16 places. Meals. Tel 562.39.41.44.
(49) Gîte d'étape de Vielle-Aure. 16 places. Meals. Tel 562.39.41.36.
(50) Youth hostel Vielle-Aure. 35 places. Tel 562.39.42.31.
(51) Gîte d'étape de Germ (also a Youth Hostel). 15 places. Meals. Tel 562.99.64.31 or 562.99.64.69.
(52) Gîte d'étape d'Adervielle. Les Amis de la Nature. On Variant 4 (see page 000). 50 places. Guardian in summer only. Tel 562.39.12.66.
(53) Gîte d'étape d'Estarvielle (near Loudenvielle). 10 places. Tel 562.99.64.12.

(54) Auberge-Refuge du Lac d'Oô. 30 places. Meals.
Tel 561.79.12.29 or 561.79.34.95.
(55) Refuge d'Espingo. CAF. 75 places. Meals. Open 1/6 to 30/9.
Tel 561.79.20.01.
(56) Gîte d'étape des Granges d'Astau. 25 places. Meals. Tel 561.79.35.63.
(57) Gîte d'étape du Moulin de Fos. 18 places. Meals.
Tel 561.79.44.51.
(58) Refuge de l'Etang d'Araing. CAF. 53 places. Guardian in summer only.
Tel 561.96.73.73.
(59) Gîte d'étape d'Eylie. 15 places. Meals. Tel 561.96.76.81.
(60) Gîte d'étape de Playras. On the Tour du Biros. 15 places.
Tel 561.96.77.14.
(61) Refuge des Estagnous. On an old route of the GR 10. 50 places.
Guardian in summer only. Tel 561.96.76.22.
(62) Gîte d'étape de Rouze (near Couflens). 15 places. Meals.
Tel 561.66.95.45.
(63) Gîte d'étape de Saint Lizier d'Ustou. 18 places. Meals.
Tel 561.96.52.43.
(64) Gîte d'étape d'Aulus-les-Bains. 15 places. Meals.
Tel 561.96.00.49 or 561.96.02.21.
(65) Gîte d'étape de Mounicou. 16 places. Tel 561.64.87.66.
(66) Refuge de l'Etang Fourcat. CAF. On the GR 10 A (see page 000).
24 places. Guardian in summer only. Tel 561.65.43.15.
(67) Gîte d'étape de Goulier. 20 places. Meals. Tel 561.64.81.84.
(68) Gîte d'étape de Liers. On the Tour du Massif des Trois Seigneurs.
16 places. Tel 561.96.94.67.
(69) Gîte d'étape de la Freyte. On the Tour du Massif des Trois Seigneurs.
20 places. Tel 561.05.94.95.
(70) Gîte d'étape de Bourgaille. About 1¼ miles (2km) from Saurat. On the
Tour des Massif du Trois Seigneurs. 15 places. Meals. Tel 561.05.73.24.
(71) Gîte d'étape de Mérens-les-Vals. 45 places. Meals. Tel 561.64.32.50.
(72) Chalet des Bouillouses. CAF. 35 places. Guardian in summer only.
Meals. Tel 68.04.20.76.
(73) Gîte d'étape du Mas La Cassagne. About 1¼ miles (2km) east of Mont
Louis. 25 places. Meals. Tel 468.04.21.40.
(74) Refuge du Ras de la Carança. 20 places. Guardian in summer only.
Meals. Tel 468.97.05.15.
(75) Gîte d'étape de Mantet (1). 18 places. Meals. Tel 468.05.57.59.
(76) Gîte d'étape de Mantet (2). 16 places. Meals. Tel 468.05.60.99.
(77) Gîte d'étape de Py. 15 places. Meals. Tel 468.05.58.38.
(78) Gîte d'étape d'Escaro. 14 places. Tel 468.97.01.47.
(79) Chalet-Refuge des Cortalets. CAF. 85 places. Meals. Hotel-restaurant
open only in summer. Tel 468.96.36.19.
(80) Gîte d'étape de Vernet-les-Bains. 32 places. Meals. Tel 468.05.51.30.
(81) Gîte d'étape. Las Illas. 15 places. Meals. Tel 468.83.23.93.
(82) Gîte d'étape. Chalet de l'Albère. Col de l'Ouillat. Meals.
Tel 468.83.62.20.

Note that unguarded cabanes and similar shelters have not been included in the above list.

There are youth hostels in the following large towns and cities in the vicinity of the Pyrenees:

(1) Gelos, near Pau. 10 places. Meals. Tel 559.06.53.02.
(2) Lourdes. 100 places. Meals. Tel 562.94.00.66.
(3) Tarbes. 58 places. Meals. Tel 562.36.93.63.
(4) Saint-Girons (about 2 miles(3.2km) from the town). 90 places. Tel 561.66.06.79.
(5) Toulouse. 66 places. Tel 561.80.49.93.
(6) Perpignan. 58 places. Tel 468.34.63.32.

* * *

BIBLIOGRAPHY

(1) *Walks and Climbs in the Pyrenees* by Kev Reynolds (1983). Cicerone Press.
(2) *Mountains of the Pyrenees* by Kev Reynolds (1982). Cicerone Press.
(3) *Classic Walks in the Pyrenees* by Kev Reynolds (1989). Oxford Illustrated Press.
(4) *Pyrenees High Level Route* by Georges Véron (1981). Gasfons-West Col Publications.
(5) *Walking in France* by Rob Hunter (1982). Oxford Illustrated Press (hardback) or Hamlyn paperback edition (1983). Useful information on all aspects of walking in France.
(6) *Classic Walks in France* by Rob Hunter and David Wickers (1985). Oxford Illustrated Press. This includes a chapter on a section of the GR 10 from Larrau to Arrens.
(7) *The Elf Book of Long Distance Walks in France* by Adam Nicolson (1983). Weidenfeld & Nicolson. This has a section on the GR 10 from Saint-Jean-Pied-de-Port to Arrens. It includes a good account of the Basque country and the Basque way of life.
(8) *A Series of Guidebooks to the Pyrenean Mountains for Walkers and Climbers* by Arthur T. Battagel. Published by Gastons-West Col Publications.
   (i) *Pyrenees West. Larrau to Gavarnie Cirque.* 2nd edition 1988.
   (ii) *Pyrenees Central. Gèdre to the Garonne Gap.* 2nd edition 1988.
   (iii) *Pyrenees East (Formally Andorra Cerdagne).* Includes the Ariège, Andorra, Cerdagne, Roussillon, Cadí and Pedraforca. 2nd edition 1989.
(9) *The French Pyrenees* by John Sturrock. (1988). Faber & Faber. Tourist guidebook which provides useful background information.
(10) *The Pyrenees* by Roger Higham (1988). Columbus Books. It describes a motoring tour of the French and Spanish Pyrenees, but provides general background reading on the various mountain areas and adjacent towns and cities.
(11) *Off the Beaten Track: France.* Edited by Martin Collins (1988). Moorland Publishing Co. Ltd. Includes chapters on Aquitaine and the Midi, including the Pyrenean regions contained therein. Written from the point of view of the foot traveller.
(12) Michelin Green Guides. General tourist information. New editions 1988. In French.
   (i) *Pyrénées Aquitaine (Cote Basque)*
   (ii) *Pyrénées Roussillon (Albigeois)*
   The two books cover the whole of the French Pyrenees.
(13) *Gîte d'étape de Randonnée et Refuges. France et Frontières* by Annick and Serge Mouraret. Creer. Lists some two thousand nine hundred establishments, including all those in the French Pyrenees and many in the Spanish Pyrenees and Andorra. Be sure to purchase the latest edition.

USEFUL ADDRESSES

(1) French Government Tourist Office, 178 Piccadilly, London W1V 0AL. Tel (0171) 493 3371.

(2) Randonnées Pyrénéennes, Cimes, 3 Square Balagne, B.P.88 09200 Saint Girons, France. Tel 561.66.40.10.

(3) Parc National des Pyrénées Occidentales, B.P.300 65000/65013 Tarbes, France. Tel 562.93.30.60.

(4) Edward Stanford Ltd (Specialist Map Shop), 12-14 Long Acre, London WC2E 9LP. Tel (0171) 836 1321.

(5) The Map Shop, 15 High Street, Upton-upon-Severn, Worcestershire WR8 0HJ.

(6) Au Vieux Campeur, 48 Rue Des Ecoles, 75005 Paris. Tel: 143 29 12 32. Nearest Métro station is Maubert-Mutualité. Extensive range of French maps and guidebooks.

(7) IGN Shop, 107 Rue la Baetie, 75008 Paris. Just off the Champs-Elysées. Nearest Métro station is Georges V. Complete range of IGN maps of France at 1:50,000 and 1:25,000.

(8) British Mountaineering Council, Crawford House, Precinct Centre, Booth Street East, Manchester M13 9RZ. Tel (0161) 273 5163.

(9) The Rail Shop (SNCF), French Railways House, 179 Piccadilly, London W1V 0BA. Tel (01891) 515477 (information only) (0171) 495 4433 (bookings).

* * *

PRINTED BY CARNMOR PRINT & DESIGN, 95-97 LONDON ROAD, PRESTON, LANCASHIRE